The Teacher of Young Children

By the same author

The Teacher of Young Children

Alice Yardley

Principal Lecturer in Education
Nottingham College of Education

Citation Press · New York · 1973

Published by Evans Brothers Limited
Montague House, Russell Square, London, W.C.1

Citation Press, Library and Trade Division, Scholastic Magazines, Inc.
50 West 44th St., New York, New York 10036

Library of Congress Catalog Card Number: 72-95336
Standard Book Number: 590-07326-5

Cover photograph: G. D. Hales

Printed in Great Britain by T. and A. Constable Ltd., Hopetoun Street,
Edinburgh.

PRA 3180

Contents

Introduction

Demands made on the teacher of young children are ever-increasing. It isn't so much that her role is changing, as that the many functions she has served in society have now gained popular recognition. Revised knowledge of children and of the way in which they develop and learn is widespread, and many things that good teachers did for children because they were sensitive to their needs, they are now expected to do.

To gather what knowledge and understanding he can of the world is, and always has been, the child's curriculum. The traditional view of the teacher as a dedicated person who knows better than parents how to help the child in this task is no longer complete. Society now acknowledges the total and individualistic nature of the child's learning. Full recognition is given to the fact that what affects the child affects all he does and that each child learns in a unique way. The complicated nature of education is comprehended and the teacher's job takes on many new dimensions.

In addition to her responsibility for the full range of work included in a rapidly expanding curriculum, the teacher is now expected to provide compensatory education for children from disadvantaged homes, to cater for the special needs of immigrant children, to have some knowledge of the problems of handicapped children, to develop firm educational links between school and home, to participate in the training of students and to work as a member of a whole team of social welfare workers.

In order to work effectively and retain her personal equilibrium, the teacher needs to evaluate these various demands and work out her own order of priorities.

In this book the more important of the teacher's functions are examined through the work of practising teachers. While the names of children and adults mentioned are fictitious, each incident or description is taken from a real situation.

Reference is made to the findings of research workers in this field, and I am most grateful to librarians in the Nottingham College of Education for their generous and invaluable assistance in helping me to identify many of the works to which readers are referred.

1

My teacher

The focal point of the young child's life in school is his teacher and to have a teacher he likes matters more to him than anything else. Well-designed buildings and good equipment improve the morale of the teacher and help her to do her job, but the child's demands on his physical environment are minimal compared with his emotional and social needs. If his teacher is right, he can adjust to almost any situation.

The simplicity of the child's view of his teacher contrasts sharply with the view taken of her by adults in the community. No one questions the importance of the teacher's job, yet few would care to define her role. Indeed, too rigid a definition would militate against the nature of the job, for the role should remain essentially as individual as the person who fills it.

A school exists and functions as a social establishment, and the person appointed to fill the role of a teacher is expected to behave according to rules which seem appropriate within that society. In other words, society defines a set of norms which become applicable to all people fulfilling the role of teacher. But the teacher is also an individual person and the way she interprets the rules makes her behaviour unique.

Society in general expects the teacher to establish a suitable atmosphere in which learning can take place, to get to know her children as individuals and to select that from which they shall learn, to develop their powers of communication so that she can impart knowledge and skills in order that they, in due course, can contribute as individuals to the community. Fundamental to the process of education in school is the teacher's ability to control both the children and the situation in which they learn, and to lead her charges towards self-control. She is, in short, responsible for their intellectual, social, emotional and physical growth during the time the children are with her in school, and is expected to pay some attention to their spiritual growth as well.

The way in which a teacher performs these tasks and fulfils her responsibilities is determined by two major factors: the kind of person she is and the circumstances in which she operates.

Mrs A and Mrs Z work in a school which receives children from generally favourable homes. Mrs A is a warm-hearted, generous woman, whose outgoing nature evokes a ready response in others. Her classroom is filled with excited interest. Her children are readily and deeply stirred, and the enriched emotional experiences they share with her are made evident in the quality of their creative work. Children normally feel happy and secure with Mrs A, yet when conflict or misfortune arise, these tend to become exaggerated. Life in her room is always a little larger than reality, yet she is well loved by children, and parents speak warmly of her. At the end of the year her desk is covered with small gifts, and children have been known to weep at the thought of leaving her for a new teacher.

Mrs Z is an intelligent woman with a keen sense of humour. Children working in her classroom are often deeply absorbed in some intellectually challenging pursuit. She expects children to work hard, to give of their best, and to accept the discipline of a chosen job before they can gain satisfaction from it. Ingenuity and originality are characteristic of the children's creative work. Children rarely cry in this room, but on the other hand they rarely get over-excited. At the end of the year Mrs Z's children show a considerable measure of self-confidence and independence, and look forward eagerly to fresh adventure in a new class. Parents respect Mrs Z and often seek her advice on how to deal with idiosyncratic behaviour in their children. It is her former pupils who in their adult life bring Mrs Z the unexpected present.

In her first post, Miss F felt very conscious of her inexperience. She was the youngest member of staff by nearly twenty years and her vitality seemed almost indecent. The high ideals she brought with her from college soon disintegrated, and she tried without much success to imitate the more experienced but less enterprising work-habits of her colleagues. The way in which she tried to teach was not in keeping with what she believed to be true about children, and many days were dissipated in an abortive attempt to control the children and keep them occupied. She was unhappy, and as her self-confidence drained away, she became more and more withdrawn.

A local organiser, who was responsible for the supervision of probationers, sensed the cause of Miss F's problems, and when a suitable opportunity arose, had her transferred to another school. Miss F's new school was in a difficult area and there were many immigrant children in her class. The head mistress, a vigorous and resilient person, was anxious to experiment with new ways of providing compensatory education. There were two other probationers on the staff. Miss F felt immediately that her ideas were sought and respected, and that her willingness to try them out was welcomed. With new-found confidence, she could face the possibility of making mistakes without being daunted, and she tried out with considerable success some of the techniques she had sampled during her training. This success and the feeling that she was accepted restored her self-assurance, and by the end of the year, in spite of the problems she faced in such a difficult school, many signs of professional competence could be seen in her work.

A number of other factors likewise influence the way in which a teacher functions in school. A woman teacher dealing with 10 to 11-year-old boys may very well evoke a chivalrous response from them, whereas the same boys would prefer to treat a male teacher as a good-humoured companion. Until recently, the Infant School has been the exclusive domain of the woman teacher whose intellectual challenge is softened by comforting maternalism. Now a few men are finding their way into Infant classrooms, where they add a different kind of excitement to the role of Infant teacher.

Age too has its effect. Small children welcome the young and inexperienced teacher for her vitality, even though the temptation to 'play her up' may have an unsettling effect on them. As the years add to her experience, the same probationer may lose some of her youthful vigour but gain in confidence and technique and find that children more readily feel secure with her.

The well-qualified teacher feels able to meet her colleagues with confidence. Problems are brought to the teacher of wide experience. The teacher who is a recognised authority in some special field, even though it may be outside the range of her teaching—as for instance the teacher who is a tennis champion—commands respect from others in the school community. In short, each particular characteristic of the person has its part to play in determining the teacher's role.

The nature of modern society adds to the teacher's problems and makes her role even more difficult to define. Technological advancement affects the teacher in at least two clearly defined ways. We teach in a world of rapid change and no longer know the future for which we are preparing our children. Our only hope is to ensure that they become flexible in their learning and able to adjust readily to unexpected demands. Tony, who is six and is already showing an aptitude for mathematical ideas, may well need to change his job two or three times before he reaches retirement age. Elaine, or John, or Ricky may not be allowed as adults to work for more than four days a week, and we need to educate them for leisure as well as for work. Brian's father is a mechanic whose repetitive job may soon be taken over by a computerised machine, and the days when son followed father in a job are gone.

Modern technology makes itself evident in the classroom as well as in the wider world beyond. Modern audio-visual aids are increasingly becoming recognised as a means of extending the child's experience. Present-day Infant teachers who stress the importance of person-to-person relationships in the teaching situation tend to be suspicious of mechanised aids to learning. But young student teachers are fast growing accustomed to technological aids. Many of them own tape-recorders and are rapidly learning to handle closed-circuit television. They are growing up with teaching machines as well as radio and television, and teachers of tomorrow will need to take notice of this gadgetry and by understanding it discover its possible benefits to the child.

In an industrial society such as our own, great respect is paid to production. The worker who participates in some profitable industrial enterprise gains more respect than the teacher, who is regarded by some as a non-worker. Only closer links between home and school can help parents to understand the demands made on a teacher in her job. The mere sight of a teacher neighbour returning home before 4 o'clock can be enough to annoy the tired housewife whose husband will be 'hard at it' until 7 or 8. The need for a long vacation is by no means easily comprehended by the man who works a continuous fifty weeks each year.

The role of the teacher in society has always been invested with problems, and although the nature of these problems has changed, it is probably true to say that the teacher of today enjoys a more favourable standing in the community than in any other age.

Early learning, even in most modern societies, begins in the home. The infant child learns about the society in which his family operates from his parents, brothers and sisters and from other members of the family. He learns by responding to what is expected of him in the way of behaviour, through imitation, and sometimes from intentional instruction on the part of an adult who is responsible for him. It is in the family and the life of his neighbourhood group that he learns how to become a social being; that is, he learns the rules and cultural habits of his immediate group in order to belong to it. The child entering school brings with him the experiences of childhood, and these are used as the basis on which to graft learning in school.

In primitive societies the infant child learns in much the same way, and what he learns depends on the cultural beliefs and way of life in the tribal community. He learns alongside members of his family and in close contact with other members of the community, and he assimilates the language, religious beliefs, skills, tribal customs and folklore of the tribe to which his family belongs. Schools as such do not exist and the pre-adolescent child continues to learn from the people he knows well. With the onset of adolescence, boys in the tribe are initiated into the adult life of society. The occasion is usually marked by tribal ceremonies, and he may be introduced to respected elders from neighbouring tribes. He is then given more formal instruction in the traditional ritual of the group and he learns of its history and aspirations. The emphasis remains on the socialising process and little specific attention is paid to the process of learning how to do a job as an adult. The type of education we offer young people in our schools is virtually non-existent in primitive societies, and learning in the early years is not regarded as an investment in the future economy of the tribe.

Girls in primitive societies depend entirely on the process of socialisation for their education, and Margaret Mead, in her fascinating study *Coming of Age in Samoa*, describes the way in which each child in the group is 'disciplined and socialised through responsibility for a still younger one'. While boys are relieved of the care of the young at 8 or 9, little girls take on the added burden of child-minding until they are strong enough to work on the plantations. Even in later life they are given only limited opportunity to acquire the skills of the group. Girls 'maintain a very nice balance between a reputation for the necessary minimum of knowledge and a virtuosity which would make too heavy demands'. She avoids spoiling her chance of marriage by being labelled lazy and inept, but is otherwise content to do routine tasks.

The idea of an adult who had specific responsibility for the education of the young was slow to emerge. In Biblical times we find the man who can record, the scribe, recognised by the group as an educational leader. The prophet is not only the teacher of religion, but also of the moral and social rules of the group. Priests of the temple are instructors; the Rabbi is the teacher of the people. In Jewish homes the father is responsible for educating his son along rigidly prescribed lines according to rules laid down in the Torah.

There was a time when the poet was respected as an educator; Homer conveyed to the people of ancient Greece his ideas about what makes a man of quality. Amongst our earliest recognised educationists, Plato, with his vision of an elitist society, endures. The philosophers of his time were the keepers of knowledge, and it was they who revealed truth and brought enlightenment to man. The schoolmaster did exist in Ancient Greece, but his was a very humble role consisting mainly of giving tuition in basic skills, and he was certainly not entrusted with the moral education of his pupils. Plato, incidentally, believed that girls should have the same education as boys. 'The same education which makes a man a good guardian will make a woman a good guardian: for their original nature is the same.' (From Plato: *The Republic*.)

Ancient Rome bred soldiers and farmers, and the father reigned supreme over his family. He taught and passed judgement on everyone belonging to his household. When schools did appear in Rome they were modelled on those which existed in Greece.

During the Middle Ages education was controlled by the Church and the educated clergy became the schoolmasters. Although education was mainly concerned with preparing boys for the priesthood, a few schools existed in which the children of laymen could receive instruction in Latin, the Bible and singing, and one can imagine the chanting of Latin verbs and passages from the Bible, as well as hymn singing, in an age when the recitation of the spoken word was what constituted learning.

In this twilight age of education a few schoolmasters emerge as great teachers, and the ideas of Thomas Aquinas and Peter Abelard are still greatly revered. St Thomas Aquinas based his teaching on the belief that 'God loves all existing things', and Peter Abelard held the theory that Christ moved men to love and repentance, thus effecting their salvation.

Modern ideas about teaching and the role of the teacher stem from the philosophy and practice of Comenius, who was a Moravian bishop. He passed much of his life in exile, part of which he spent in England. Regarding education as a means of social regeneration, he saw the need for the child to learn through immediate experience. Modern classroom procedure with its picture books and visual aids originated in his attempt to make education realistic and not entirely dependent on verbal communication.

Rousseau, Pestalozzi and Froebel saw the child as the focal point in the educational situation, with the teacher working alongside as provider and guide. Dewey's ideas on education were based on the needs of society and he saw the process of socialisation as the process of education. Children learned by being placed in problem situations, and he regarded teachers as participants in the child's adventure into learning.

In pre-industrial Britain it was considered dangerous to educate the masses, but the sons of the aristocracy received formal tuition along carefully structured lines in classical languages and literature. Knowledge was comparatively stable and was transmitted to pupils who accepted it as unchanging and sacrosanct.

The industrial development of Britain brought radical changes. Society needed literate and numerate people, and schools were established to provide elementary education for the masses. The teachers who emerged as a result of the implementation of the 1870 Act were expected to produce at least a prescribed level of competence in all pupils. Payment by results was introduced as a means of ensuring cheap instruction for all in the basic skills of reading, numbering and writing. Children were educated for an occupation and most of them re-mained in the same occupation throughout adult life. The teacher knew precisely what to teach and how to teach it. His role was limited but clearly defined, and he was expected to accept a mere pittance for his efforts.

Modern practice and the role of the teacher still suffer from many of these influences. Parents who were brought up to regard tuition in literacy and numeracy as dominant in education find it difficult to adjust their ideas to the changing needs of society. Many teachers still see instruction in the three R's as their main function, but there are others who, while recognising these basic skills as important, view them as a mere part of the total pattern of learning. Teachers today are alert to their responsibility to the child as an individual who can with their help make a unique contribution to society, and see their job as a means of helping him to become what it is he has in him to be.

This change in emphasis has been slow to emerge, and many years may pass before the pendulum stops swinging and the appropriate function of schools and teachers reaches a state of equilibrium.

2

Research and the role of the teacher

Comparatively little research has been done on the role of the teacher in the modern Primary School. Teachers who are interested in studies made in this field will find a list of references in an appendix to this book. In evaluating this material it should be noted that until very recently few schools could claim to be working in a completely spontaneous and creative way, and the clinical study of children and their teachers in this kind of situation has yet to be made.

Perhaps the most outstanding source of enlightenment and understanding of the teacher's role is the work of Dorothy E. M. Gardner and Joan E. Cass, who studied the way in which teachers were working in Infant and Nursery Schools over a number of years. Their findings are published in *The Role of the Teacher in the Infant and Nursery School* (Pergamon Press, 1965).

In this study attention is focused on what teachers actually do when children are engaged in periods of freedom to choose their own activities. Detailed records of the interaction between teacher and child illustrate what constitutes good and successful teaching in informal education. An analysis of the contacts made by some teachers showed that they covered every aspect of the primary school curriculum during the course of informal activity. It was often difficult to distinguish between 'giving help' and 'showing care for comfort' on the part of the teacher. 'Help at one moment to one child might be a gift, the building up of a relationship, but for another child the withholding of help might be an assumption of the ability to be independent and might therefore be the more positive approach, though less obvious as such to the observer.'

The report contains many interesting findings. Good teachers clearly attached great importance 'to the need to co-operate closely with the ideas and plans of the children'. All teachers were 'actively concerned with the provision of adequate material and its care and use'. They were invariably warm and friendly and encouraged children to be helpful and friendly in return. They accepted without hesitation the role of leadership and 'responsibility for guiding the child to good social behaviour and sensible attitudes towards work'. Suggestions and advice predominated over positive commands, but good teachers did not hesitate to intervene in order to improve the quality of the child's learning. While teachers remained generally aware of the dangers of 'getting children on' without due respect for the stage they had reached in development, each teacher felt clearly responsible for ensuring the maximum development possible for each child.

In his study *The Role of the Teacher of Six and Seven-Year-Old Children*, (Manchester, 1967) C. L. Baird analysed the classroom activities of twenty teachers working in five Infant and five Infant/Junior Schools. Ninety per cent of the sample spent the major part of their time and effort in catering for the intellectual development of children. Their contribution to emotional development, to fostering social attitudes and to maintaining control and discipline were made in that order of priority. While 'no significant differences in score were found between inexperienced and experienced teachers in infant schools, significant differences occurred between such teachers in infant/junior schools'. Teachers in the Infant Schools 'used time-tables with a progressive bias', while teachers in Infant/Junior Schools used 'time-tables with a traditional bias'.

In 1964 Musgrove (Bradford) and Taylor (Leicester) carried out an extensive enquiry in Grammar, Modern, Junior and Infant Schools to establish the conception held by teachers and parents of the teacher's role. They found that 'in all types of school teachers saw their work primarily in intellectual and moral terms and were comparatively indifferent to more general social training'. While teachers believed that parents were mainly concerned with instruction, attached great importance to social advancement and were comparatively indifferent to moral objectives in the education of their children; parents, in fact, 'gave a list of educational priorities which agreed in substance with the rating made by teachers'. Parents' expectations of teachers, Musgrove found (1961), were related to social class and to their children's stage of education. Working-class parents of Primary School children, for instance, 'wished to place far greater responsibility for behaviour-training on teachers than middle-class parents, who felt that this was the responsibility of the home'.

An interesting feature of this research is the discrepancy found between teachers' aims and what they imagined to be those of parents, when in fact parents are substantially in agreement with teachers. More effective means of communication, it is suggested, might reduce considerably the area of tension between them.

The comparative study of the conceptions of College of Education students and head teachers with reference to the teacher's role was made by Finlayson (Liverpool) and Cohen (Anstey) in 1965. Widespread disparity was found between students and head teachers. Students did not on the whole appear to change their views very much during the three years of their course, and this leads one to suppose that a source of conflict facing the student teacher as he enters school as a teacher is the idealised concept of the role put over by his college tutors which contrasts sharply with the concept held by the practitioner.

A point of interest made in this research is that both groups regarded the function of social training as more important than the teaching of the three R's, and this finding is in contrast to that of Musgrove and Taylor already mentioned.

Studying the role of the teacher within the social system of the school, L. J. Westwood (N.F.E.R., 1967) examines the influence of social and cultural forces external to the school and the consequent complexity and difficulties inherent in the role of the teacher. These studies refer in general to the Secondary School teacher, but they are of considerable interest to teachers in all types of schools. Technological and social change, he points out, 'can add a cultural gap' to the generation gap and 'quite often it is the teacher who does not know what the child is talking about rather than the reverse, and age no longer automatically implies greater knowledge and authority'. He mentions the difficulties of observing teachers at work and suggests that one of the reasons why the teacher's role has not been more carefully examined 'is that intervention in the school situation is a difficult and delicate matter'. He draws the conclusion that 'the essence of the role concept is reciprocity' and that 'worthwhile research in this field will, of course, examine both pupils' and teachers' roles at the same time'.

A conclusion the reader may draw from these studies is that findings can appear to be in conflict, and that much depends on the sample used in an inquiry and on the way in which the measurement instrument is designed and presented. Teachers who are asked, for instance, to consider a set of aims and place them in order of priority may state preferences which are not always reflected in their classroom behaviour. A teacher may emphasise, for example, her function as instructor in basic skills, while in practice she is spending a great deal of her time and energy in maintaining order in the class. Another teacher may stress the importance of creative work and the development of individual personality, but these depend very much on how far she can establish a good social environment.

Meanwhile teachers and children continue to work towards some solution to many problems, and there remains here a vast unexplored area for the future research worker.

3

The image of the teacher

There was a time when it was believed that because children were young and less knowledgeable they were less intelligent, and hence that the person responsible for their upbringing needed little in the way of intellect. There are, indeed, still many people—even some who are responsible for education in this country—who hold the opinion that the more intelligent teachers should be reserved for older children, while those who are less academically gifted 'would do quite well with young children'.

Recent research into children's thinking emphasises the extreme importance of early intellectual development. The quality of thought and reasoning at later stages depends considerably on the way in which the foundations of conceptual development are catered for.

The child of five or six is unable to explain his thoughts to his teacher, for he has neither the vocabulary nor the sentence structure with which to convey his ideas and impressions in verbal terms. His teacher must be intelligent enough to understand what is going on in his mind long before he can tell her; her own mind must stimulate the minds of fast developing children—and some of those children will be very intelligent indeed.

One of the greatest joys in teaching is the knowledge that somewhere along the line a teacher has been able to help an intellect which is better than her own. And the teacher of young children can meet, in a child as young as five or six, an intellect which she recognises as superior.

The image of the motherly Infant teacher, whose job it is to love and look after young children, is fading, and that of the vigorous and intelligent woman who understands young children and has a deep and genuine concern for their welfare is taking its place. She is a person who has undergone a full course of training and is qualified because she has passed successfully a number of rigorous tests. Many teachers of young children have undertaken an extra year of advanced work for which the Bachelor of Education degree is awarded. The teacher's professional skill and intellectual capacity have been confirmed before she enters the classroom.

When the man in the street considers the teacher's job, his images are rooted in his own early experience. He may realise that times have changed, and features in the press or on films or television may attempt to enlighten him about the way in which children learn in the schools of today, but his personal experience of new ways of thinking and revised classroom procedure remains extremely limited, and teachers should tolerate these difficulties experienced by parents and other adults in the community.

Clues as to the ideas others hold about the teacher's function are reflected in the way people treat the teacher.

Dave is six and has four brothers and sisters. Dave's parents find the odds against them overwhelming, and his mother sent the following note to Dave's teacher: 'I sent our Dave off yesterday, but he's been truanting again with that lot from Crocus Terrace. If you don't stop him at it he'll have to be put away. He takes after his father and there's nowt I can do.' Dave's parents have abdicated and his teacher is expected to take over and act as a parent substitute.

Mary's father visited the classroom on Parents Day. He complained to Mary's teacher that she 'wasn't getting on'. The teacher showed him ample evidence of Mary's ability, but Mary's father persisted: 'She can't be learning anything. She says she loves school and enjoys it all day. When I was at school we hated it, but it learned us.' His impression of a worthwhile teacher was based on the instructor of his early days, and the idea that Mary should enjoy learning was quite incomprehensible.

Frederick brought his teacher a passion flower. 'My father says there is a story about this flower,' he explained: 'He said ask you because you're a teacher and you should know.' Even the intelligent parent sometimes expects the teacher to be an infallible source of knowledge.

Disgruntled passengers on a corporation bus complained: 'Children have no manners nowadays. I don't know what they teach them in school.' They clearly held the teacher responsible for the good manners of other people's children.

The Plowden Committee detailed an alarming array of responsibilities associated with the teacher's job. She must 'take responsibility for the full range of work in a single class', and her 'training should overlap more than one stage of education'. She should be conversant with individual and active methods of learning, while remaining aware of 'the need for practice of skills and consolidation of knowledge'. Essential subjects for the Primary teacher are R.E., English, mathematics, art and craft, P.E., history, geography and environmental studies, together with sex education and social education. She should be prepared to teach English to immigrants, to work in priority schools, to help handicapped children and to work alongside a teacher's aide. She should understand the social factors that affect school performance and be familiar with the structure and function of the social services. Fostering the co-operation of parents and readiness to develop the school as a community centre are also considered to be essential parts of her job.

A teacher who attempts to fulfil the many roles designed for her by other people will end up in a state of permanent conflict. It is important that, from the outset, each teacher should create her own self-image; knowing herself and what she can offer, she must decide what she would like to be as a teacher. The establishment of this idea of self will help her to discriminate between conflicting demands. It will provide, too, the foundation of personal conviction, and the teacher who is doing what she firmly believes to be the best under the circumstances is able to withstand the adverse criticism of others when things go wrong.

Initially, the teacher's idea of herself as a teacher is linked with her reasons for entering the profession. Some people enter because they 'love' children, but soon discover that just loving children is not enough, and that knowledge of children and the ability to understand them and view them objectively is a more helpful attitude. Some power-loving personalities see in children the opportunity to dominate those younger and less knowledgeable than themselves. Others enjoy a platform and regard children as a captive audience. Some enter the profession because their parents have decided they shall, and may see the training as an inexpensive means of extending personal education. Few enter the profession because it offers high financial rewards.

However, the majority of people who are interested in becoming teachers of young children have a genuine desire to help them. They have sympathy for the young learner and a sincere interest in him as an individual.

Initial motives may not persist, and many teachers who entered against their own wishes, or for the wrong reasons, have discovered an unexpected interest in the job and a growing fascination in the study of the developing child. More than one teacher has decided to teach in an Infant School because the hours are shorter and it seems the least of the evils. Those who have stayed there have been won over by the children, and one rarely finds a teacher of five- or six-year-old children who is out of sympathy with them. For the unsympathetic person the job becomes impossible and she doesn't stay in it.

Present-day methods ensure that teachers of young children live very near to their charges. The classroom becomes an essentially human situation—varied, intensely interesting and largely unpredictable, The teacher is a person who is persistently faced with problems, many of which she is unable to solve. It is as well to recognise this fact from the outset, for the teacher who regards herself as a problem-solver is working under an illusion. No one can devise universal rules to meet the very varied situations which unexpectedly confront a teacher, and the teacher of young children is thrown back on her own resources time and time again. She does what she can in all sincerity, and she may never know whether the problem has been solved.

Teachers do not work miracles with disturbed children overnight. The treatment a child receives from a teacher may help to alleviate his problems, but the idea that a temporary relationship with her, however salutory it may be, can rectify some deep-seated disorder is quite fallacious. Yet we still find teachers who would have us believe that 'Anita', who on entering school was completely withdrawn, inarticulate and antisocial, is now a happy, communicative and friendly individual as a result of the treatment she received from her teacher.

Although many problems met by teachers in school are insoluble, this does not mean that the teacher can do nothing about them. She tries and she may be rewarded. On the other hand, it may be that a teacher at a later stage in the child's career will reap the benefit.

Sometimes older teachers meet as adults children they once taught. What is remembered by the adult of his early relationship with a teacher can seem unbelievably trivial, but the very fact that it remains means that it made a lasting impression and therefore effected a degree of change in the developing person.

What do we remember of significant relationships in childhood? That a certain adult loved colours, was exciting when he talked about birds, awakened our interest in the way man uses tools? Sometimes we know from the young child himself what it is he appreciates about us, or how we influence him. We will do well to take note of the way the child views us, because this is our surest guide to the role we play.

Mike's school was in an educational priority area. He was always first to arrive and could not be persuaded to stay away even when he was ill. He said little, but one day a sudden burst of feeling enabled him to express his appreciation of his teacher. 'I like you, Miss,' he confided: 'I like you because you smell nice.' Knowing his mother, the teacher quite understood.

When Rex entered school his new teacher was in her probationary year. At the end of the first week his mother asked him, 'Well? Do you like school, Rex? Do you like your new teacher?' Rex nodded enthusiastically; 'She's smashing,' he said: 'She takes us out on the playground every morning.' He paused and then added, 'But you know, Mum. She's only a big girl.'

Janice enjoyed school from the first day. She described each day's events to her mother over tea. One evening she was most excited, 'Our head teacher's got a father,' she announced: 'And I've found out who he is.' 'Oh!' said Janice's mother: 'Who is Miss B's father then?' 'It's God,' Janice declared: 'When we go into the big hall we put out hands together and Miss B says, "Dear Father God".'

Many children believe that their teacher exists only in school. The idea that she has a mother, a father, perhaps a husband or a child, may seem quite incredible, and the fact that she gets paid for being there is frequently regarded as unbelievably funny.

Children are compelled by law to come to school. The teacher is free to choose whether or not she shall work there. She need not put up with the children, but they must suffer her, and this situation reinforces her responsibility to them.

4

The personality of the teacher

In school the most educative part of the child's environment is the teacher, and what sort of person she is affects him most profoundly. On entering school the child is still very dependent on the adults who take care of him, and he is therefore readily influenced and willing to appease the person who can satisfy his needs. His happiness and well-being depend on the approval he receives from his teacher. This makes her a very powerful person and she can, if she so wishes, mould the child into becoming what she wants him to become.

The hallmark of a good teacher is her ability to put the interests of children before her own. She recognises and respects the individual nature of each child, and she resists the temptation to 'mould' him. She is first and foremost concerned about helping him to become a person—in his own unique and inimitable way. Her best contribution to his full personal development lies in the inspiration of her own personality; she cannot avoid influencing him, but she does it through what she is rather than by intention. The child sees in her the pattern of a mature and responsible person who is willing to guide him while leaving him free to develop a personal pattern which is entirely his own.

What the child most needs to find in his teacher, as a person, is someone who is willing to share with him all aspects of life. She supports and encourages him without being over-protective. She establishes a happy environment for him, yet never pretends to him that life is completely happy. She helps him to set for himself realistic goals and to select tasks which he can hope to accomplish, but she allows him to encounter a degree of frustration and disappointment because she knows their value as stimulants to further effort.

A mature and whole person knows that wholeness in personality is only achieved by living life at all points. Joy is only recognised by those who have known sorrow. Compassion is earned by those who have learned to sympathise with the troubles of others. To experience the heights involves a person in accepting the depths. It is while the child feels secure in the loving care of those who are genuinely concerned about his welfare that he is able to meet fear, unhappiness and disappointment. These are experiences which will make all the difference between living in a dull, flat and two-dimensional way and living in the fullest sense of the word, as a person who is prepared to experience all that life can bring.

Knowledge of the child's need for security, especially during his early days, has led to considerable misunderstanding of what is best for the child. Some adults would cut children off from half of life's experiences, and these same adults are shocked when a child expresses an interest in suffering, fear or death. But children are naturally curious about all aspects of life. They are quite ready to face frightening situations, and will learn how to adjust to and cope with them if the right kind of adult stands by. The parent or teacher who is over-anxious will prevent the child from embarking on the full adventure of life. Who is to blame if the child becomes a weak or shallow person, or one who pretends that life is one great, safe wave of happiness? A courageous and full-living adult will invigorate the child and help him to feel free to experience and express the full range of his impressions of life.

The child's sense of security stems more from the emotional balance of the adults who are responsible for him than it does from his physical environment. Many of our children come from homes where parents live in conflict with one another and with their surroundings. Home is a cluttered, disorganised environment which offers neither peace nor privacy for the individuals in it. In homes such as these there is no place for personal possessions, nowhere to hide a present in readiness for someone's birthday, no place one can call one's own. Even the lavatory may offer little in the way of privacy if it is shared with other tenants or with two or three neighbours. Children from such homes need to meet an adult who can maintain a measure of serenity, even when a situation is trying. Children whose lives are turbulent are often difficult in their behaviour, and they need to find in their teacher a person who can remain undisturbed by this behaviour. To be near a person who is at peace can have a more calming effect than anything else on an upset child.

Sometimes, in busy classrooms, conflict is inevitable and things may get out of hand. The teacher who can move quietly amongst the children, speaking perhaps to the individual child will allay the conflict more effectively than the teacher who shouts for silence.

Serenity is a quality which is difficult to acquire and maintain, but which is well worth working for. It is the basis of mental health, and it is on the mental health of the teacher that that of the children in a class depends. Each person has her own means of maintaining personal equilibrium. Some find it through absorbing pursuits outside the classroom; some find it through ever-deepening interest in their study of children; others find it in their quest after spiritual development, and yet others through a homely concern for the people they meet in the course of daily life.

Teaching is a great challenge to personality, for the immaturities of children bring out the immaturities of their teachers. Many teachers feel threatened by the gifted child. Behaviour in children which irritates the adult offers a clue to that adult's own weaknesses.

A teacher's sense of values is an essential aspect of her personality. Her attitude to books, music, poetry, works of art, natural phenomena, personal relationships, religion, etc., is of great importance. The child's powers of discrimination are largely undeveloped and highly flexible; since the teacher is the child's introduction to important adults outside the home, what she thinks can influence him profoundly. The education of taste is as important as any other aspect of the child's development. He can learn much through the teacher's example without being dominated by her choice.

The teacher who allows the child to see what she feels about things, and who shares with him the experiences which matter to her, enables him to catch a glimpse through another person of what is most meaningful in life. Only the best is good enough for children, and by showing the child what she considers to be the best, the teacher can help to establish in him a sense of values. Even the child who comes from a home where things of value are fully appreciated has much to learn from an adult outside the home. In school he is freed from the limitations which may be imposed on him by the attitudes of people at home.

In the modern classroom the relationship between teacher and child is a very intimate one indeed. In this close human relationship personality is the vital factor, and because she is a person outside the home environment, the child's teacher can awaken aspects of his personality which may remain unmoved in the home.

John, for example, had a good home which offered him the opportunity to develop spiritually as well as physically and emotionally. He was clever and his academic education was well advanced before he entered school. His ability to write was used by some of the children when they were trying to record their experiences. 'John can write it down for us,' they said: 'We'll draw the pictures of the policeman and what he told us about when he came.'

John obliged by writing down what the children said, but he avoided paint and never attempted to draw a picture. One day his teacher suggested, 'Why don't you make a picture about the trees we saw in the park? The colours were lovely and you could use paint or some of this pretty material.'

John shook his head. 'I can't draw,' he said: 'I can't make

things look right. Daddy's no good at drawing. He shows me how to write things down, but he can't show me how to draw.' Even at the age of five and a half John was becoming a perfectionist. Because he was clever, much was expected of him at home, and his immature attempts to draw were considered poor. What he couldn't do well he didn't attempt.

'Very well,' his teacher agreed. 'Don't worry about making the shape of the trees. Just choose the right colours from the box of material and stick them on the paper. It isn't easy to tell me about the colours in words. You can write the rest.'

The idea appealed to John. When describing colours, fabrics were more adequate than words, and his colourful record of the autumn trees pleased him. During the following weeks he 'illustrated' many of his descriptions with blobs of paint or scraps of fabric, and his writing became more imaginative. Fresh aspects of his personality were awakened, and he began to free himself from the limitations of the need to do everything 'exactly right'.

There is no blueprint for the ideal personality pattern of a teacher. Children enjoy the sunny nature of a vigorous outgoing young person; they appreciate the sensitivity of an imaginative and creative person; they respect the inspirational qualities of a person with high ideals; and they love the warmth of a great-hearted, homely woman. They are most perceptive as regards sincerity, and the person who is able to remain herself and at her best under any circumstances endears herself to children, even though at times they may find her a difficult person to get on with.

Perhaps the most severe test of personality for the teacher is the kind of relationship she makes with the children. How to influence them without requiring them to conform to her sense of values, and how to put their needs before her own self-satisfaction, are the most difficult challenges a teacher may have to face. The relationship between teacher and child should enable the child to develop his individuality in a way which is entirely his own. He should be liberated in the relationship rather than bound by it, and, because of the support the relationship provides him, his delight in adventurous living should be intensified.

Great educators have always recognised this rigorous demand made on the teacher. Even when instructional methods of teaching set her in an all-powerful position, the personality of the teacher was usually more influential than her authority. With the skill of a true artist, Herbert Read expresses this aspect of her role in the following words:

'Teaching demands a high degree of asceticism: joyful responsibility for a life entrusted to us, which we must influence without any suggestion of domination or self-satisfaction.'

(From *Education through Art* by Herbert Read. Faber.)

5

The teacher as a specialist in children

A young probationer was flattered—and a little worried—by the faith parents seemed to have in her knowledge of children and of family matters.

'Our Jimmy's had me up all night with pains in his stomach. What do you think it can be?'

'This is me youngest. He'll be a year old tomorrow. I've told me hubby he's got to be the last, but he's a healthy man and he'd have me breeding like a rabbit. What would you do with him?'

'Young Judy here's been at it again. She stuffs herself wiv biscuits every time me back's turned. She's bin like this ever since the new baby came and I haven't the time to be watching her. You're a teacher. P'raps you can do somefink about it.'

The fact that the teacher was unmarried and barely twenty-one seemed irrelevant. The parents expected her to be an authority on nervous disorders, physical disabilities, intellectual idiosyncrasies, marriage and family planning. These were the skills expected of any teacher put in charge of their children; after all, she had been trained for the job.

In the early part of the century the teacher was expected to acquire at least a modicum of knowledge which could be used over and over again. She taught by instruction, deciding what the children should learn and how they should set about it. She rarely exposed her knowledge to the unexpected question from a child, because she was the one who asked the questions and was only prepared to accept the answers she already knew.

Today the child is the agent of his own learning. His teacher introduces him to worthwhile situations, but his approach to them is individualistic and he learns what is appropriate for his stage of development. It is *his* interest rather than the teacher's which leads the way. If the teacher's material is good and well presented, the child will ask many questions. He will not wait to ascertain whether his teacher has taken a course in science or astronomy or physics; he asks the awkward questions which come into his mind, and sometimes the teacher finds the situation embarrassing.

There has been a drastic change in the role of the teacher over the last fifty years, and the fundamental reason behind this change stems from our ever-increasing knowledge of the child and of the way in which he develops and learns. The idea of children as being semi-filled vessels ready for topping up would seem quite ridiculous to the teacher of today, because clinical observation of children has shown the need to understand the child and the nature of childhood before we can hope to help him to learn. Learning must fit the child.

Present-day teaching is based on knowledge of children, and a study of the individual child is a prerequisite of the job. Research workers make fresh discoveries hourly, and the child development course taken during initial training needs constant revision, for the teacher must keep up to date with the findings of modern research workers in this field.

No teacher today is short of information. Every woman's magazine runs articles on child care and psychology. Television programmes describe experiments in vivid detail. Lectures by eminent educationists are available to all. Visiting inspectors and specialists urge new procedures on the practising teacher. Even the local organiser or educational official is well primed with a pet educational theory.

Unfortunately, because our knowledge is still in its infancy, experts offer conflicting views. The teacher who readily accepts each fresh idea presented to her is torn apart and may become a danger to the children she teaches. A sense of personal conviction is a teacher's means of survival; it is the measure by which she assesses the advice offered to her. If this ever-increasing volume of information is to be of use to her, she must be selective.

Conviction is not something which can be taught to students in training. It is part of personality and grows as personality grows. It starts when a student is allowed to see that others possess it. Conviction is a personal guide, and to witness it in another person is an inspiration.

What we select to make our own depends on previous experience. Something makes sense because it clarifies what we have already partially discovered, and we can accept fresh information which fits into the existing pattern of our own personal development. This is the test of what we can work with, of what we can absorb and make our own. We pay careful attention to each fresh idea, neither accepting nor rejecting until we have put it to this test.

In this way conviction begins to develop. It is conviction based on knowledge and understanding, which enables teachers 'to exercise judgement' and 'to think on their feet'. (Plowden, para. 875.) There are no rigid rules when dealing with the human situation, and a teacher cannot prepare to deal with events in a classroom by learning a set of rules in advance. Understanding a child offers clues as to his behaviour, and knowing why he behaves as he does helps a teacher to deal with him in a beneficial way.

Knowledge of children reveals a very wide range of behaviour within the normal pattern, and this helps a teacher to accept as normal much that she might otherwise resent or worry about. Acceptance of a child is her first step towards making a helpful relationship with him, and it provides a channel of communication between her and even the most difficult child. She is then able 'to make children feel that they matter, however little they are able to respond and however unattractive they may appear to be'. (Plowden, para. 873.)

Knowledge of the patterns of human development enables a teacher to know what to expect of a child and when to expect it, and to realise that individual differences between children mean that what they learn and the rate at which they learn varies widely. She will not expect each child to respond as she herself does to a situation; she can then respect his individuality, even when his interests clash with her own.

Most important of all, her study of the child will cultivate in her the ability to remain detached from him and take a clinical view of him as one child in relationship with others. This is one of the teacher's greatest assets. Parents are inevitably emotionally involved with their children and find it difficult to take an objective view of them. They may expect too much of a child, or too little; they may see him as they would like him to be and not as he is; they may want him to become like themselves, or someone he is not. The teacher may be the first person beyond the home to see the child as he is, thus enabling him to be himself. It is with vast relief that some children discover themselves in the atmosphere provided by an understanding teacher, and feel able to embark firmly along the path towards ultimate independence. The teacher can free the child in a way that parents cannot; by doing this she extends the work of parents who basically want their child to be an independent person.

Tony's father was a physically powerful individual who admired masculine qualities in men. Tony was a sensitive child, slender in build like his mother, and more interested in books than football. On his sixth birthday, Tony's father bought him a football and some football boots. 'I'm going to make a man out of you,' he said kindly enough: 'I want you to be able to stand on your own feet and hold your own.'

Tony brought his football to school and made no attempt to stop two or three little toughs making off with it. He settled happily to the imaginative model he was making of a spacecraft. 'Isn't it exciting,' he said as he worked: 'You can fly to the moon in this and one day I'll be an astronaut and find a new planet.'

Tony went home without his football. When his father came to enquire about it, his teacher explained: 'He forgot it. Your son has intense powers of concentration and he's absorbed in trying to understand space travel. He is imaginative too, and I think he could become an inventor or a scientist.' Tony's father looked surprised. 'You mean he's bright?' he asked: 'He's never shown much interest in things I ask him about, but then I haven't much of a head for science. I wonder where he gets it from!' Tony's father wasn't converted on the spot, but a start had been made.

Becoming a specialist in children enables a teacher to be articulate about her job. A teacher should be able to explain to a parent why she has adopted a particular way of organising her classroom. She needs to be able to explain her views on educational theory to other members of staff, and to be able to tell inspectors how she hopes to develop a new interest in her classroom. And, as she becomes more competent in her job, she needs to be able to describe her aims to members of an education committee and put before them her case for promotion.

Being articulate means speaking well and with understanding of the issues involved. Mere verbosity about the job is not the same thing; indeed, modern methods have suffered a great deal from the verbosity of those who do not understand them. Some of the most ardent advocates of revised methods of teaching are enemies of educational advancement, for they use words they have learned, and because the words mean little to them, they become debased. One hears teachers using such terms as: 'We do *activities* in the afternoon'; 'We have *creative* on Thursdays and Fridays'; 'We have an *integrated day* once a week'. They claim to be 'progressive', and criticisms are levelled against their misinterpretation of liberal and individual ways of working.

The wise teacher avoids using many of these terms. She uses, instead, her own words to explain as simply as possible the ideas she holds and what she is trying to do. If she understands what she is attempting, she will find appropriate words of her own with which to convey her meaning.

The study of her job and of the way in which children learn is not a task undertaken by the teacher once and for all time. The dynamic nature of education means that the learning situation is always changing, and a teacher needs to maintain the habit of day-to-day enquiry about what she is doing and why she is doing it. Theory grows out of practice, and it is the teacher of today who is helping to shape the theory of tomorrow. 'By their practical work in the classroom, teachers have perhaps as much to contribute to psychology as the psychologist to educational practice.' (Plowden, para. 518.)

Mary Brown entered her first job full of enthusiasm, and older members of the staff listened kindly while she explained the ideas she hoped to put into practice. They were experienced enough to offer what help they could and then stand by while she made her early experiments and met with some disasters.

Mary planned her activities with care and imagination, but her children remained dependent on her. 'Can I paint now, Miss Brown?' 'I've finished my books on spiders. What can I do next?' 'There's no paste left, Miss Brown.'

Mary turned for help to an experienced teacher. 'How is it,' she asked, 'that your children seem to run their own affairs? I can't make mine take over and they need me all the time.'

Her colleague smiled. 'Perhaps they don't feel responsible,' she suggested, 'because they haven't been involved in planning things for themselves. Each time I take over a new class, I spend the first three or four weeks of the term working out with the children how we shall organise and run their workshop. For example, "Where shall we put the paint easels"; "How can we make sure that when Peter has finished using his rubber apron, it will be ready for Susan to use?"; "Can you find a quiet corner where we can read our new books?" All this takes time and each group of children works things out in a different way. After all, the classroom is a workshop which belongs to all the people who work in it, and I'm only one amongst forty.'

Theory emerges from the way in which teachers view the child and his rights. Ideas about flexible forms of organisation, integrated ways of working and a creative approach to learning are not recently discovered. They have grown out of the work of teachers whose knowledge of and interest in children is based on their personal experience of them. Modern theory has emerged as a result of many years of enquiry on the part of teachers who have discovered the value of letting the child take the lead.

6

The teacher in the classroom

Mrs Jessop has a class group of thirty-five children whose ages range from four years ten months to six years six months. The school is situated in a shabby part of the city and the majority of her children come from underprivileged homes. The class also contains a few children whose parents are fairly prosperous business people in the area. It is, therefore, a mixed group, gifted in a warm social sense but generally lacking in academic ability.

On this particular morning Mrs Jessop arrives at about 8.30 a.m. and finds half a dozen children already busy in the classroom. They know that they have access to many activities and materials but that some tools are locked in the teacher's cupboard until she arrives.

The children set to work as soon as they enter the classroom. Some finish off jobs they started on the previous day. One child arrives with an idea about a picture he wishes to make; another brings a collection of boxes from which he hopes to construct a garage. Others explore familiar situations such as water, sand or bricks, and a few wander round the room until an object or, perhaps, fresh material suggests a new line of investigation.

It is a wet day and, as the children take off their wellingtons, Mrs Jessop helps them to peg their boots together in pairs. There is much discussion about pairs, twins, double, bicycle, duet and other expressions meaning two. Some children want to know why feet are different in shape, and why people take different sizes in shoes. They cut pictures of shoes from magazines and paste them in rows on a sheet of card to represent, in simple graph form, how many children in the class take each size. Wet socks are draped over a radiator. Some socks are made of wool, but many are made of nylon yarn or cotton. The time taken by each type of fabric to dry is noted and the children want to know 'why the nylon is the quickest'.

At half-past nine Mrs Jessop remembers the register. She finds she can check it without calling for silence and asking the children to answer their names, as she has already made contact with each child present. She checks her marking against the milk bottles in the crate—for each child has, on arrival, slipped a tag bearing his own name around a bottle of milk. By the end of the morning all but a few of those bottles will be empty, and the children who have not yet had their milk will be reminded by the monitor in charge.

For most of the morning Mrs Jessop moves from group to group. She has developed the ability to cater individually for more than one child at the same time. She can, for instance, supervise Tommy, who is learning to fasten the laces of his plimsoles, while she writes down a sentence for Barry beneath his picture of the robot story he watched on television the night before; she manages to keep an eye on the experiments which a group of children are making at the investigation table, and, at the same time, listen to the discussion that is going on about the size of shoes.

From time to time she gives more systematic help to a small group of children who are anxious to 'read the story by themselves', or to some children who are preparing labels for the 'Things we have made' display.

Individual records of what the children achieve are an important part of Mrs Jessop's job, and today she is concentrating on the progress each has made in his powers of classification. She notes that Don and Rex are sorting bricks according to their shape, and that Sarah is anxious to take this a stage further by adding size to the criteria. She notices that, for the first time, Judith has offered to sort out the make-box and is carefully grading the lengths of ribbon as she packs them away.

Mrs Jessop doesn't forget Paul and Mike who have asked for 'a turn with the dressing-up in the hall'. They are trying on headwear in front of a mirror, and as they don a policeman's helmet or a king's crown, they become for the moment an imaginary character. Near by, a group of children using chime bars provide musical accompaniment for the little drama. The whole experiment is very fluid and crude, but at this stage the teacher leaves them to work things out for themselves. Later they may wish to repeat both drama and tune, and they will need her help in shaping and writing these down.

At about 11.45 Mrs Jessop says, 'I have set the pinger clock for ten minutes, and when the alarm sounds we should have a tidy room'. Before the children get ready for lunch there is time to share a song and a well-loved poem.

These activities are resumed in the afternoon, and the big 'pack-away' for the day is timed for about 3 o'clock. After this, all the children collect informally on the 'story carpet' and discuss the events of the day or listen to a story.

Mrs Jessop then shows the children an example of Jacobean glassware from the display of 'Things made of Glass', which she promises to set out for them the next day. 'I hope you will enjoy my glass—but just with your eyes to begin with,' she says: 'This glass jug is very old and not very strong. I'm very fond of it and I want you to enjoy it too, but it would break very easily. There will be some things you can pick up and I'll show you which they are.'

In Mrs Jessop's classroom most days follow a similar pattern. Long unbroken periods of time enable children to become absorbed in a pursuit, to start a job and finish it before moving on to another. In a flexible programme there is always time to take up an unexpected interest, and the arrival of the man with the big bag of coke just outside the classroom window offers a teaching point and is not an interruption.

On some days, 'movement' takes place in the hall at a

fixed time. The children know when to expect this and may even set the alarm clock to warn them when to change and go into the hall. Otherwise there are few breaks in the day. 'Playtime', as such, disappeared long ago, because it did not compete favourably with the excitement of the classroom and often interrupted what the children were doing.

If Mrs Jessop were responsible for children of eight or nine, the basic pattern would remain but would undergo some fundamental adjustments. The children would work more often in small groups than individually, and the groups would form round some particular interest or material. These groups would be more permanent than those of younger children, and would take on the structure of working parties in which individual children were allocated jobs which suited them. There would also be a period set aside each day as 'Teacher's time', when the teacher would take over and decide where systematic practice of a skill was required. By this stage the children would understand the use of skills and would be prepared to take an interest in perfecting them. Practice in the skills of reading, creative writing, music making and handwriting, the extension of the child's ability to calculate and to classify, and the crystallising of discovery in a particular aspect of the environment are some of the many jobs allocated to 'Teacher's time'.

The older children would also be capable of sustaining their interest over several weeks, of organising their own library or film club or, perhaps, a carol-singing expedition. They would be well advanced in the development of basic concepts, and would be approaching a stage when abstract thought opens up opportunities for them to reason and follow logical argument.

The function of the teacher changes according to the stage reached by children in conceptual development, but at every stage the teacher's job involves her in preparation, presentation and communication and in ensuring progress for each child in his learning.

Preparation begins with the assembling of objects and materials to provide effective starting-points in the classroom. The child's curriculum is his discovery of all he finds in the world. His life's job is to understand his surroundings and make adjustments to them; survival depends on his ability to control his environment, and in order to do this he must first learn about it.

The classroom is 'an environment contrived for children's learning' (Plowden, para. 548), and the teacher's preparation is a matter of selecting from the child's world those situations which are likely to be of greatest use to him. Her choice depends considerably on her own interests, and things which interest her offer a personal link with the child. These are the things about which she is most knowledgeable, and her own enthusiasms will arouse enthusiasm in the child.

Interests can range from cooking, gardening or sewing to deep-sea diving, rock climbing and archaeology. A collection of objects which the children can handle and observe will link each child with these pursuits and provide the opportunity for first-hand discovery. This personal contact will form the basis on which to construct a body of knowledge.

Providing the stimulus of a suitable environment is not, however, enough. The teacher should know in advance the possible lines of enquiry which can arise in any situation, and she will then be able to further the self-chosen interest of individual children. She will know in advance the most helpful reference books to suggest, the most appropriate piece of equipment to add to an exploratory situation, or the question which will stimulate the child's thoughts.

The way in which a teacher introduces her material is also part of her preparation. The impact of a full display, arranged overnight by the teacher, is only one means of sparking off interest, for this may also arise as a result of some object brought by a child, or from a single object shown to the children; or perhaps, as described in the following incident.

It was winter. Water was frozen and snow stood deep outside the classroom. The children placed a board on the snow and fed the birds with scraps of fat and bread. This simple event excited great interest, and when the children came into school they chattered freely about what birds eat, how they keep warm, how they are able to fly and why they don't sink into the snow when they stand on it. Their enthusiasm opened up several avenues of investigation, and their teacher provided further opportunities for observation of bird habits. She also made sure that many kinds of material were available and that each child chose his own means of conveying his impressions.

The effects of such experiences, and of displays of objects which stimulate interest and curiosity, involve the child in communication, and communication introduces the use of basic skills. The child exchanges his impressions with others through speech and through representation in the form of picture, model or drama. As his skills develop he learns to record in written form and to extend his discoveries by reading books. Along with the materials displayed, the teacher provides many modes of communication, and children learn to become articulate in speech, paint, clay, wood, movement and mime before they learn to communicate by means of written words, numbers, notes and other visual symbols.

At every stage the teacher's most influential contribution to the environment is a well-furnished mind. Learning for the young child is largely a social activity, and intellectual enquiry is stimulated by the sparking-off of mind against mind. Many children have an intellectual capacity which remains virtually dormant within the life of the home. Their first teacher may represent their first encounter with a mind which can challenge their intellectual qualities. In the early years of a child's life the growth of the mind is rapid. It is not too late during his first years in school to open up his intellectual life, even though it has been previously neglected.

Closely associated with a challenging mind is the teacher's capacity to listen. The adult who stimulates thought and speech in a child, and then listens while he attempts to communicate thought in the shape of words, is the child's most effective educator. The teacher who can stimulate questions on the part of the child, and then listen to him when he tries to think aloud in search of answers to his own questions, is the most powerful intellectual challenge the child can have.

7

The teacher as an organiser

One of the most difficult problems facing the probationary teacher is that of classroom organisation. Even experienced teachers face each new class with a degree of apprehension, realising the importance of the first few weeks of the year in establishing the way in which teacher and children will work together.

Much depends on the framework around which the work of the year will develop, and in this country class teachers are given a considerable amount of responsibility. Few head teachers attempt to tell an individual member of staff how her classroom should be organised and run. Provided that she fits in with the general methods of working employed in the school, the class teacher is usually left to plan her own scheme.

This is a great privilege and, at the same time, a great responsibility. The well-organised class appears to run easily, and the more informal the way of working, the more important the organisation becomes. Freedom for all means accepting the limitations which allow others to be free. The freedom to choose from a wide range of activities means that each activity is disciplined to fit in with the rest. Modern classroom procedure is based on a form of well-disciplined freedom, and there are many ways of creating the freedom in which individuals can work at peace with one another. Jean Weston's experiences illustrate one approach to the problem.

The school in which Jean was to spend her probationary year was built in 1932. The classrooms were designed to accommodate only thirty children and they stretched in a long row, flanked on one side by an enclosed veranda. French doors on the other side opened on to an asphalt space, beyond which a shrubbery separated the school from the neighbouring estate.

Jean's activities started a week before the beginning of term. She surveyed her classroom, where the caretaker had arranged dual tables neatly in rows. It also contained storage cupboards with sliding doors let into the wall, a few storage bins on wheels, two mobile bookcases, a clothes-horse, a large table-topped desk for the teacher, and two low free-standing cupboards; in one corner there was a large sink.

Jean was expecting to have thirty-six children, aged between five and six, in her class. She persuaded the caretaker to remove six of the tables and then she rearranged the furniture to allow for a space in the centre of the room, with the tables arranged in pairs in different parts of the room to provide large working areas. The top of her own desk provided an additional working space. She used all the mobile furniture to define a number of bays and, with two bookcases, she created a reading corner which offered some privacy from the rest of the room.

On the following day the headmistress issued stationery, brushes, paint and other consumable goods from the store. Jean asked for bricks, some clay and a sand tray, which were found for her. She was told, however, that there was not enough equipment to enable her to have a house corner in her classroom, but that there was a spare room equipped for house play, dressing-up and music making, which served all six classes in the school.

Jean was anxious to explore the 'mathematical dimension of domestic play' described by her maths tutor at college. She ransacked her mother's kitchen for small-sized kitchen equipment, and with this she created a well stocked, if shabby, domestic play centre in her own classroom. She filled the storage bins with exciting waste materials and treasured pieces of fabric. From the clothes-horse she suspended tin lids, a triangle, some cups, flower pots with a rope knotted through the base, and other objects which children could tap with a wooden spoon and so experiment with music making. She used the corridor space outside her classroom door for painting and woodwork.

During the next few days Jean made little books of all shapes and sizes in which the children could draw or write; she stapled sheets of kitchen paper together to make large painting-books, and collected magazines containing attractive pictures of people and places which the children could cut out.

She then turned her attention to the register, for knowing the names of her children in advance would help her to identify them more quickly when she met them. She bought a packet of strong cardboard tags and wrote each child's name in bold lettering on one side, and she screwed thirty-six small hooks into a peg board in six rows of six.

Remembering what she had been told about involving the children in the organisation of their workshop, she surveyed the room. She felt that she had provided a range of starting-points to which she could add activities, materials and situations as they seemed appropriate.

The cardboard tags proved a success. As the children arrived she gave each one a tag bearing his name and suggested, 'If you draw a picture of yourself on the other side, we shall all know which name belongs to you. If you hang your name on one of these little hooks when you arrive in the morning, we shall know who is here and who is away. When you want to know how to write your name you can find it on the tag.' Later Jean found many mathematical ideas could be illustrated by the arrangement of these tags: for example, simple graphs using a variety of criteria such as colour of eyes, amount of pocket money, number of pets, and so on.

Jean's good start was short-lived. As the children became familiar with their surroundings trouble arose. Most of them crowded into the house corner or scrambled for a stand near the sink. Jean panicked. How did a teacher allow free choice when all the children wanted to choose the same thing? Jimmy provided a clue.

'It's not fair, Miss. I want a turn in the sink with the hose you can see through and that lot's had it all morning.'

'We'll have a list for taking turns,' Jean suggested: 'You can sign up on the list but there's only room for four at a time.'

'Yes,' Jimmy agreed: 'And nobody can have another turn until we've all had a turn.'

Signing up on the list provided an added incentive to the mastery of writing one's name, and rotas appeared for paint, the house corner and bricks.

Some activities remained unpopular. 'I can't understand,' Jean complained to another member of staff, 'why my children aren't very interested in clay. Yours make some lovely shapes and models with clay.'

'Do you like clay yourself?' her colleague enquired. Jean's first reaction was, 'What's that got to do with it?', but by the end of the first fortnight she noticed a close correspondence between the things she enjoyed and the activities which were popular in her room. She had introduced an investigation table, and that had gone well from the start; mathematical and scientific interests she found absorbing, and the children were obviously affected by her enthusiasm.

'What is it about clay I don't like?' Jean wondered: 'I avoided it in college when I could.' She picked up a lump. It was hard and difficult to handle. She tried to work a little water into it, and the surface grew slimy and oozed through her fingers. She opened a fresh polythene container in which the clay was packed and extracted a lump. It was firm, yet elastic, and responded readily beneath her fingers. Her hands slipped round it.

Two little girls were staring at her. Then they fetched aprons and joined her. 'Can we have some out of the bag?' they asked.

Fifteen minutes later a small group of children were silently absorbed in the responsive material, and, as Jean watched their fingers at work, she began to appreciate the educative value of clay. Clay was a material she would need to rediscover with the children.

'Miss Weston, there's no scissors,' Philip complained: 'I want to cut out a picture for my book about mountains and there's no scissors.'

Jean examined the box. Twelve pairs of scissors had disappeared in about the same number of days. If she continued at this rate, she thought, she'd either be charged by the Local Authority or she'd be spending half her salary replenishing her stocks.

'Everybody must look for scissors,' she decided: 'We've lost twelve pairs and we must turn out all the boxes and cupboards. They must be found.'

The children co-operated enthusiastically and within ten minutes the room was in chaos and five pairs of scissors had been retrieved. A pair found in the wastepaper basket indicated how the other missing pairs had disappeared.

'We could have hooks,' Philip suggested, 'and hang them up like our names.'

'All right,' Jean agreed: 'When it's time to pack away you can check up, Philip, to see that the scissors are all back on their hooks.'

Half the term was gone before Jean felt confident in the way her room was organised. Fortunately she had a sympathetic headmistress.

'It may take you two or three months,' she explained, 'to come to an understanding between yourself and the children. Take your time because it's time well spent. Try to make sure that the children know exactly what you expect of them. Treat anti-social behaviour as a mistake and show the children quite clearly that they are responsible for keeping the classroom in order. It's the children's business to clear up the floor at the end of the day, not yours or the caretaker's.'

Jean's patience and persistence were gradually rewarded. She discovered that many children enjoyed being methodical, and the less tidy-minded individuals in the group were disciplined by their friends. The children were on her side and felt responsible for the smooth running of their workshop. It was theirs as well as hers.

It is much easier to do things for a child than to train him to do things for himself, and the test of good organisation on the part of the teacher is the capacity of the children in her class to work independently, asking her advice and help only when problems are beyond them. The young child's struggle towards independence is part of his effort to survive, and the adult who helps him to become an independent being is loved and respected by him.

The way in which a group of children work together usually reflects the habits of the teacher. If a child opens the cupboard in which the teacher keeps her property and is greeted by a cascade of pencils, paper, paste pots, flour, crayons and paper clips, he is not encouraged to establish order in his own tidy-box. Many teachers have discovered the value of training themselves to acquire orderly habits, even though such habits may not come easily to them.

Organising the classroom workshop sets the scene for learning, but this is only the start; planning for progression and ensuring meaningful activity on the part of each child are major aspects of the teacher's responsibility. When planning an activity the teacher may start in a modest way, keeping in reserve material which will promote further exploration once the child's interest has been stirred.

The teacher, for instance, who understands the characteristics and behaviour of water might promote exploration in the first place by providing a range of bottles, a funnel and a jug for pouring. Later she will add, one by one, squeezy bottles, transparent tubing which enables the child to observe the relationship between air and water, a syringe, tins with holes pierced in either the bottom or the sides, and so on. Each additional piece of equipment is calculated to take the child a step further in his discovery.

Where children work as individuals and are encouraged to develop many different interests, careful records of each child's development are essential. Many teachers keep a notebook on hand in which to jot down any significant incident as it occurs. Much is lost if observation is not recorded on the spot. The notes can be entered in the child's individual record at a later date. The following page from a teacher's record-file indicates the way in which she observed one of her children during his first days in school.

Mon. Jan. 8th. Martin admitted. Very quiet and withdrawn. No one has heard him speak but older sister says he can. Cannot hold a pencil, but dabbed a little with a paint brush. Did little else.

Wed. Jan. 10th. Martin spoke. He said 'No' when I said we were going into the hall for service. He hid under my desk and I left him there with Julia (aide) keeping an eye on him.

Fri. Jan. 12th. Martin made his first relationship. He fought with Sheenah for the possession of a paint brush.

Tues. Jan. 16th. Martin smiled. He fastened his own coat buttons and I said, 'Well done, Martin! You are a clever boy with your buttons'. I have come to the conclusion that Martin has too much done for him at home. He has two older sisters, and his grandmother is left in charge of him while his mother (widowed) goes out to work.

Fri. Jan. 19th. Martin scribbled with a pencil, in much the same way as a two-year-old child would. He brought the results to show me and seemed very pleased with his 'picture'. I mounted it and pinned it on the wall. Martin has made his first step towards becoming a social person in school. He should learn a lot from working with other children who treat him as an equal and don't merely mother him.

8

The teacher as a member of a staff team

The school community consists of a large number of children and a few teachers, together with a number of other adults such as the caretaker, the secretary, the teacher's aide, lunchtime supervisors, the cook or kitchenhand, and so on. Where a true sense of community exists between these people, conditions for learning are created, and the children can learn from one another and from every adult in the group. Other adults who form part of the child's educational environment join the group from time to time, and organisers, students, college tutors, HMIs, publishers' representatives and tradespeople can contribute in various ways. Parents, of course, can make an essential contribution to the child's education in school.

The young child may tend to cling to 'his' teacher, but as he gains social confidence he will make increasing use of other adults in the group. Many schools organise the child's environment in a way which enables him to encounter as many different people as possible. People are the most challenging part of his environment, and the school which centres education on the needs of the child bears this clearly in mind.

The community takes its lead from the headmistress, who is the leading teacher in the staff team and who is responsible for establishing a way of life which offers adequate opportunity for each member of the community. Her personal philosophy affects the whole community. Even so, she is extremely dependent on each member of the group and, in particular, on each adult in the group. Where the staff team is concerned, each teacher in it matters, and team-work depends on the personal characteristics of individual teachers.

Reliability is, perhaps, the most important quality required of a teacher. Few things are more destructive of staff morale than the person who lets others down, who stays away from school and leaves others to look after her children when she could really make the effort to be present, who is never around when it is her turn for playground duty, and who avoids helping the child who is sick or who had dirtied his pants. Members of staff will tolerate much in the way of incompetence if a person is conscientious and can be trusted to fulfil her responsibilities to the best of her ability.

Loyalty could come next—loyalty to other members of staff and to the head. A teacher may be tempted to discuss the shortcomings of others on the staff with people outside the school, sometimes with parents or visiting inspectors. The opportunity to add to one's own stature by diminishing the contribution of another is not always easy to resist, particularly when a teacher feels insecure. Where members of staff are bound together in loyalty, the unity of a school community is assured, and few qualities are more obvious to a person who visits a school.

The willingness to share ideas leads to co-operative ways of working. Some teachers tend to hoard their ideas, fearful of the success of others who take them up and develop them, but team-work means that ideas must be exchanged and shared. Ideas are dynamic, and sharing them with others helps them to grow.

A sense of humour is essential in the teacher of young children. Children have a unique and unpredictable way of reacting to situations, and very often the best laid plans of the teacher fall apart. The most exciting schemes can prove fruitless, and the ability to admit disaster and take it, along with success, as an important part of experience, will prove invaluable.

Maintaining a sense of perspective becomes increasingly difficult towards the end of each term or when important events are pending, and the member of staff who refuses to get worked up about trivial irritations can have a very beneficial effect on distraught colleagues. A cheerful person is a great advantage to a staff, and a person who can laugh at herself helps others to reduce problems and misfortunes to their proper size.

There are many other desirable attributes in a teacher, and perhaps one other should be emphasised. Personal honesty leads to personal integrity, and the unpretentious person who remains herself under any circumstances is universally accepted by the group. Few things are more irritating on a staff than the teacher who tries to dazzle her audience with false pretences.

Flexible ways of working make teaching today an intimate and very personal job. What happens in a school depends on the nature of the team in charge of things, and a noticeable feature of team-work is the way in which it changes as a result of the personalities who contribute to the group. Head teachers who believe in democratic forms of leadership agree that if a member of staff changes, the effects are evident throughout the school. 'It's like changing the ingredients in a cake,' one headmistress explained: 'By changing the recipe, a cake can become madeira sponge or rich fruit cake.'

The way in which individual teachers affect a group becomes evident in most schools at the time when children go home. From some classrooms children emerge a few at a time, chattering to one another and helping those who have problems with buttons and laces. Another door opens and children march out in a single file, maintaining a disciplined appearance until they reach the end of the corridor; once they are out of sight of the teacher they shed her authority like a restrictive coat, and their repressed energy bursts upon any companions within reach. Still further along the corridor, a door bursts open and children seethe out in an unruly mob. Their teacher flaps along with them, still struggling with Freddy's mackintosh belt which seems to be twisted round and round the loops which should hold it to the coat; Daphne is sobbing because her hands are cold and she's lost her gloves, while Mark hobbles slowly behind with his wellington boots on the wrong feet.

In this situation, two members of the team are destroying the harmony of the school; one because she is authoritarian and the other because she is completely disorganised and unable to help her children to develop their powers of self discipline.

The characteristics of a class group reflect very clearly the characteristics of the person in charge of them. One teacher watches anxiously for petty pilfering and seems to foster it by paying it too much attention. Children in another class are tale-bearers. One unhappy group seems to contain more than its fair share of neurotic children and more cases of absenteeism than any other.

On the other hand, attendance in the class of another teacher is always high, and curiously enough these children seem to fare better even when measles or chickenpox sweeps through the school. The creative and academic achievement of this group is sound, but not perhaps so spectacular in quality as the achievements of children in the classes run by the authoritarian teacher or the neurotic one.

Teachers usually foster in children the qualities they themselves believe in. Children tend to give what is expected of them, and if the emphasis is on perfect handwriting and neat, grammatically correct sentences, they will strive to please their teacher by producing these. If, however, a teacher feels that the emotional and social development of children is as important, or even more important, than academic achievement, she will tend to have a happy sociable group of children whose creative work is spontaneous and delightful rather than technically competent.

In this way each teacher affects the group of children in her care, and these together make up the total community.

But teachers affect one another as colleagues in ways which are equally observable. While the most influential person in the team is, of course, the headmistress, the staff group can be coloured most forcibly by any one of its members.

Miss Thomas, as a probationer, joined a staff of experienced teachers. While she was in no way outstanding, she had a genuine interest in young children and was anxious to try out some of the ideas her college had recommended. Her main concern during her first term was about her ability to 'manage the children'. She watched with admiration the ease with which her next-door neighbour, Mrs Kay, handled her class and noticed how even the most difficult child responded when Mrs Kay made a suggestion.

She expressed her approbation. 'You make it look so easy,' she said to Mrs Kay: 'Could you give me a few hints? I think the children like me but I'm afraid they'll get out of hand, and I feel I'm holding them down all the time.'

Mrs Kay appreciated the approval of her junior. 'That's not a bad way to start,' she said: 'Better than letting them get on top of you. I'll come in when you're ready to clear away. That's the testing time and perhaps I'll be able to make some suggestions.'

Miss Thomas's sincere appreciation was extended to other members of staff. She openly admired Mrs P's exciting room and the lovely display of shells in Mrs W's room. 'She's a nice little thing,' they told one another: 'Not like some of those young things who come out of college thinking they know it all and ready to put education to rights.' They enjoyed her approbation and felt better for having her amongst them. Miss Thomas, in turn, received support from her colleagues and the benefit of their experience. When she made a success of things they were as pleased as she was; when she made mistakes they were tolerant and withheld their criticism.

The greatest acknowledgement came from the oldest member of staff. 'She's like a breath of fresh air about the place,' she said: 'You've a lot to learn, my dear, but you're a good learner and I'm glad you came here. Now do you think those young legs of yours could chase after that Russell Preston of mine? He went out to draw a plan of the playground and he's been gone long enough to dig it up.'

When Miss Thomas disappeared the others agreed. 'We were getting a bit set in our ways,' they admitted: 'Some of her questions make you think about what you're doing. We needed a bit of vigorous young blood, and perhaps we'd better think about having another youngster when we open the new class next term. She needs a companion of her own age and we need waking up a bit.'

The employment of teachers' aides in the classroom is another dimension of team-work. In some schools aides are available to class teachers for perhaps one or two days each week, while in other schools each teacher has the full-time services of an aide. The way in which aides can work as part of the staff team depends on the type of person appointed as an aide and the way in which the school is organised. From the point of view of the individual class teacher, the relationship needs skilful planning, and not every probationary teacher feels confident enough to work alongside a second adult who may be a mature and forceful person and a powerful influence amongst young children.

One young teacher, however, found her aide a tremendous help during her probationary year. The aide had worked in the school for some time and the headmistress had allocated definite responsibilities to her. Her main job was to maintain and replenish consumable equipment, to attend to sick children, to deal with classroom problems at the teacher's discretion and, most important of all, to listen to children and talk to them about their immediate interests.

The aide was a warm-natured woman, motherly without being dominating. She helped the young teacher to arrange her room and organise her equipment, and offered suggestions when they were invited. Her only weakness was her tendency to gossip, and the young teacher learned to cope with this by saying 'I mustn't hold you up, Mrs B. Susan would like you to staple her pages together, so I'll have to hear the rest some other time.'

In every situation one factor emerges: the need for each member of staff to work within the pattern of the whole school. In even the most formally organised school, a class unit is not contained within the four walls of the classroom. What happens within that unit affects the whole school, and the total pattern of the school impinges on the unit. Where classroom doors stand open, or in an open-plan building, this factor is emphasised even more.

Each member of staff has some particular strength. One teacher may have a flair for display and creative work; another may understand electricity and be an excellent cook, while a third may be inspirational in movement. In the flexible school of today there is easy communication between individuals and between class groups, and the children have access to the gifts of each member of staff. Team-work involves each teacher in offering her gifts to the whole community, thus assuring the fullest possible enrichment of the child's environment.

9

The teacher and authority

The teacher can view the concept of authority in at least three different ways: in order to qualify for the job, the teacher must become a figure of authority; her job places her in authority over the children; at the same time, she acts as a tool of authority. Each of these aspects of her role affects the relationship she has with the children in her care.

An important aim of a college course is to make the teacher an authority—an authority on children, an authority in some chosen field of study, and an authority on the general curriculum which the child is expected to cover. This initial course of training is followed up in most Local Authorities by a series of in-service courses, for the ever-changing nature of education means that the teacher in action is always re-learning her job.

We have already considered the need for the teacher to communicate with children through her own strengths, and her success in the classroom situation depends very much on the way in which she furnishes her mind before she enters it. As an authority on the material she presents to children, she becomes a challenge and an inspiration to them. As an authority on children she becomes a person who understands, and who, therefore, can accept, a wide range of behaviour and reactions on the part of individual children.

It is this acceptance of the child as he is which provides the foundation of a helpful relationship with him. This relationship is not dominated by the need of the child to placate his teacher by being what she wants him to be. He feels free to be himself and is therefore able to develop as an individual.

This same sense of acceptance enables the teacher to view each child objectively. She is not personally affronted by a child's aggressive behaviour; she isn't hurt if a child rejects her; she isn't disturbed when he becomes anti-social: she is interested in these manifestations, and her stable view of him is conducive to his mental health. He feels normal because she treats him as though he were, and the liberation of his normal self is encouraged by the sense of communion which exists between them.

No teachers in the world have more authority in running their affairs than those in this country. In many countries the State determines the teacher's political opinions, but in Britain neither the political beliefs of the teacher, nor her nationality, are barriers to appointment, and are not, in themselves, barriers to promotion. The law of the land decrees that in every Primary and Secondary School there shall be a daily act of corporate worship and religious teaching, but that no teacher will be required to give, or be penalised for not giving, religious instruction (Education Act, 1944).

Perhaps the greatest freedom allowed to British teachers is the responsibility for determining the curriculum and the methods of teaching. Local organisers and Her Majesty's Inspectors can offer advice and criticism but, providing a head teacher maintains reasonable standards and can justify her choice of action, both the curriculum and the approach used in a school are her decision. Most head teachers share this responsibility with the staff team and expect the co-operation of each member of staff in working out the philosophy and curriculum of a school.

In many schools in other parts of the world teachers are given a scheme of work and a detailed programme to which they are expected to adhere. When a child transfers from one school to another, his new teacher can be told precisely at which stage he is in his grades. The system is uniform and depends on allowing only a modicum of authority to each teacher.

So familiar are teachers in this country with this liberal

state of affairs that they tend to think of their authority in terms of discipline, or restriction on the child's freedom, rather than on their own. In schools today teachers tend to feel very uncertain about the idea of discipline. The term 'freedom' is often misunderstood, and there are even some who believe that freedom and discipline are incompatible. An examination of the terms may help to clarify the issue.

John Dewey, in his book *Experience and Education* (Collier Books, New York), makes some astute comments on the nature of freedom. 'The commonest mistake made about freedom,' he writes, 'is, I think, to identify it with freedom of movement or with the external or physical side of activity.' And again, 'The only freedom that is of enduring importance is freedom of intelligence, that is to say, freedom of observation and of judgement exercised on behalf of purposes that are intrinsically worthwhile'.

These two freedoms cannot, of course, be separated, for when we restrict the child in movement we restrict his opportunities for discovery and for intellectual growth. It does not follow, however, that by freeing the child in a physical sense —leaving him free to move about the room—we necessarily improve his opportunities for learning.

When teachers talk about 'free discipline' they mean that the child's own discipline of self replaces the discipline of him by the teacher, but the removal of teacher control does not, in itself, encourage the development of self-control. Again, freedom for one child to use paint when he has an urge to do so means that another child must restrict his use of paint to some extent. And the child who is free to give full bent to his natural impulses may find himself unhappily at the mercy of his own emotions.

What, then, does discipline mean in terms of the liberal methods pertaining in present-day classrooms?

In Chapter 7, we considered the need for a framework of law and order which enables each child to select and pursue a meaningful job and ensures the kind of harmony that is essential for a group. Complete freedom is more than a child at a very immature stage in his development can handle. Having a few essential rules, and recognising them, helps to establish a sense of security, and knowing how far he can go is almost reassuring for a young child. Many children suffer from some degree of anxiety, and the establishment of limits and of a few 'peg times' in an otherwise free day provides a stable pattern for the child. Many adults, when faced with the freedom of holiday time, choose to stay in a holiday camp, or a hotel, or embark on a cruise. They seek a form of timetabled freedom and like to feel sure when the next meal will be ready.

Some form of timetable helps the young child to develop a sense of time. All he has discovered about the world leads him to suppose that interdependent life must conform to an agreed pattern. The most natural of days needs a pattern, and a rhythmic sequence of events helps the child to feel he safely belongs to a scheme of things which has been worked out for his benefit.

The ultimate aim of the teacher is to help the child to depend on himself, and to establish within himself personal rules which will serve as a guide throughout life. A simple example will illustrate one way in which this can be achieved.

Jeremy's mother was divorced. She had a full-time job, and Jeremy had his own way with his grandmother, who looked after him during his waking hours. When Jeremy came into school he had little idea of sharing and went into a tantrum when he didn't get what he wanted. His powers of self-control were very meagre indeed, and, because he was a strong and forceful little boy, the other children tended to give in to him. In his good moods he could be completely charming and he knew how to use his charm as well as his temper. In other words, he was a likeable child in spite of his selfish behaviour, and it was usually easy to give into him.

Jeremy's teacher, Mrs Evans, avoided a battle of wills until he had a chance to settle down. During his sunny moods she asked Jeremy to do a number of jobs about the classroom.

He seemed to enjoy the approval of the other children and of his teacher, and Mrs Evans tried to develop in him good social habits by avoiding the occasions when she knew he would resist her suggestions.

The time came when she felt she must press Jeremy further, and her opportunity came when he offered to help two other children to make a book about feeding the birds.

'I'll draw the pictures,' he decided: 'I don't want to write. Dawn and Philippa can do the writing.'

Mrs Evans sat down with the three children and planned how the book should be made. 'I'll cut the pages and staple them together for you,' she suggested: 'What shall we have on the cover?' Jeremy grew impatient. 'I want to draw the bird-table and me putting crumbs on it,' he complained: 'And Philippa can put the words under and I'll show her how to write my name.'

'If you draw the picture,' Mrs Evans pointed out, 'you must do the writing yourself. You can do a page each, and then I'll put them all together to make the book.'

Jeremy drew his picture; then he left the group and went to build with the bricks. Mrs Evans fetched him back. 'You haven't finished,' she told him: 'The others have done a whole page, but yours can't go into the book until it's finished.'

'Don't want to write,' Jeremy scowled: 'I don't like writing.' Mrs Evans took no notice of the rising storm.

'You write quite well,' she said calmly: 'I shall expect you to finish your page before pack-away time.' She picked up the rest of the pages and carried them away to her desk. 'You can bring yours to me when you've finished it, and then I will put the book together.'

Jeremy stabbed at the page with his pencil, and Mrs Evans thought for one moment that he was going to scribble across his picture.

'Have you spoiled your page?' she said quietly: 'It doesn't matter. I'm sure Philippa would like to make the first page. When she starts a job she finishes it!'

Jeremy's fingers clutched the pencil and he laboriously began to shape the simple sentence. 'Jeremy,' he wrote, and then he became caught up in his own effort, 'fed the birds with crumbs.' The book was completed and put in the library corner, and Jeremy had taken a major step towards becoming a social being.

Step by step Mrs Evans encouraged Jeremy to fulfil his obligation to others in the group and to develop the sunny side of his nature. He began to accept the discipline of approval and disapproval of his companions. He was learning how to curb his own impulses and desires, and to understand the rules of social control.

Teaching is a service. The Education Act of 1944 made the parent responsible for ensuring that his child was suitably educated. The State offers education in school as a service to parents, and the teacher is a tool of this service. In this country no one is compelled to teach, and when a teacher asks to be given a job and is appointed, she takes on the responsibility of operating as a tool of the Education Authority which appointed her.

Authority takes various forms. Individuals employed in the system may take decisions which affect the teacher and the schools, but each decision is based on the law of the land. The 1944 Act established the appointment of a Minister and a Ministry of Education (now called the Department of Education and Science), and the Local Education Authorities were placed 'under his control and direction'. The Minister, now Secretary of State, is responsible for deciding policy and action, and the Local Education Authorities are responsible for the execution of his decision. Nevertheless, much is left to the discretion of the LEA, and from the teacher's point of view it is the LEA to whom she is primarily answerable. A Primary School may have a board of managers, or it may be one of a number of schools managed by the Primary sub-committee of the LEA. Sometimes school managers may seem to hold a powerful position.

The people in authority most likely to influence the class teacher are the representatives of the LEA—inspectors, organisers or advisers—and the representatives of the Department of Education and Science—Her Majesty's Inspectors. It is important to understand the function of these people, and the teacher should know what her attitude to them should be.

Nowadays, the function of an HMI is to advise rather than to inspect, and HMIs are carefully selected to act in this capacity. They bring to the job extensive experience and can be a great help to the teachers, for teachers can discuss their problems with them. They are capable of offering sound advice, and it is the responsibility of the teacher to use their experience and expertise to help her in her job. They are her friends, and will respond in a friendly and helpful way if this is what is expected of them. Approached in the right way, HMIs can be an inspiration to a school.

The local inspector may do a similar job for her own Authority. Often the local inspector or organiser is mainly responsible for the appointment of teachers and the staffing of schools. Probationary teachers are an important part of her job. Many local organisers have encouraged educational development in their area. Indeed, there are some striking examples in many parts of the country of the way in which a local organiser has furthered the cause of education.

Too often teachers destroy the benefits afforded by these people because they are afraid of them or expect them to be critical. It is very difficult for an inspector to offer advice and help when a teacher clearly expects to be found at fault and is consequently on the defensive. The teacher has, after all, been appointed as a suitable person to make decisions about the way in which she and the children should live in the classroom. What happens there is her way of life and she has no need to defend it. She may seek to improve it, but no one will expect her to change it. The way she is used as a tool of authority is decided by her own attitude to that role.

10

The teacher in society

There are people alive today who can remember the Victorian governess who turned to teaching because her family had fallen on evil times and there was little else she could do. Beyond her own meagre education, she had no qualifications for the job and she was very poorly paid. It was not until Kay-Shuttleworth pointed out that progress could not be effected in popular education until teachers were trained and qualified that the importance of the job began to be recognised. The Battersea Normal School was opened in 1840 as the first teacher training college.

For many generations society had rated the teacher very low in the scale of social values. Even when a State system of education was established, progress was hampered by the imposition of payment by results on the school curriculum. There are still many today, both parents and teachers, whose assessment of education in schools is geared to attainment in word recognition, handwriting, grammar and calculation. These lingering attitudes account for the resistance to the ideas of teachers who understand the need to encourage development in every aspect of a child's personality.

In spite of these limited views of the profession, teachers have, for generations, proved their flair for social leadership. A good example is found in the position held by the village schoolmaster or mistress. Such teachers have frequently won a position of respect in the community because of what they are and because people in the community have learned, from childhood, to turn to them for leadership.

Members of the Plowden Committee express their concept

of the teacher's role in the community in no uncertain terms: 'It has long been recognised that education is concerned with the whole man: henceforth it must be concerned with the whole family' (Plowden, para. 129). 'Together with others such as health visitors, teachers could become an important source of guidance for parents on what to do with children out of school' (para. 128). The Report also recommends that Community Schools should be developed in all areas, especially in Educational Priority Areas, and defines a Community School as 'a school which is open beyond the ordinary school hours for the use of children, their parents, and, exceptionally, for other members of the community' (para. 121).

The teacher's job is no longer understood as existing within the four walls of a classroom. Teachers are expected to reach out and concern themselves with each child's family and with the community which forms his background and within the context of which he will learn. Social education is now considered to be an important aspect of the teacher's job. The Seebohm Report on the Social Services (July 1968) emphasised the importance of the teacher in social developments. This means that the teacher is placed in a key position and can earn the respect of the society through her service to it. While this position brings recognition, it also brings added responsibility.

The status of teachers in this country has been advanced considerably by the work of professional associations. Existing associations have grown up separately, most of them originating as attempts to bring together teachers from schools of a particular type. While the consideration of common problems has benefited members of separate associations, the consequent lack of unity in the profession has not been helpful.

The largest of these associations is, of course, the National Union of Teachers, and although there are records in broad outline of the courageous attempts of this association to secure the rights of its members, comparatively little is known of its history. It might be worth mentioning that this association sponsors M.P.s on both sides of the House, thus ensuring that the interests of teachers are maintained before Parliament.

Generally speaking, professional associations have fought not only for improvement in the salaries and conditions of service of teachers, but equally for the recognition of sound educational practice and for the establishment of teachers in the eyes of the community. The present trend towards professional unity must surely add strength to the work of the associations.

Plato saw education as a means of producing men who were capable of acting as guardians of the State, and he advocated popular education, the teacher's job being to train the young to become good citizens. Education was for the service of the State, and he felt that the interests of the individual were satisfied by the fulfilment of duty to the State. Plato and his colleagues thought deeply about education, and their theories form the foundation of Western educational philosophy.

Today a considerable percentage of the national economy is spent on education. Society invests in its own future by educating its young, and the present-day view of education is that it should do two things for the child: firstly, it should help him to understand the society in which he is educated and help him to fit into it; secondly, it should develop him as an individual and so equip him to contribute to society and help to develop it. Society pays the teacher to attend to these things and has a right to expect its demands to be met.

Recent research in child development has helped to stress the needs of children, and education is centred on our understanding of the child as an individual. The Plowden Report emphasises the idea that 'the best preparation for being a happy and useful man or woman is to live fully as a child' (para. 506).

Nevertheless, we do not fulfil our responsibility to society unless we remember that the child grows up as an individual within a social group and that he needs to accept the pattern of his society before he can contribute to it, or attempt to change it in any way. The child inherits a wealth of traditions and cultural values, and his teacher is responsible for helping him to understand his own society and for handing on to him the cultural wealth which is his birthright.

In terms of classroom experience this means that the teacher should acquaint the child with the best in English literature, drama, music and art. He should learn about the customs of his country and the beliefs held by the people in it. He should understand and respect the work of his forefathers, the beauty and majesty of the countryside, and the quality of thought which has gone into the architecture of the country's finer buildings. He should be made aware of his environment and of the lives of people in it, and he should be brought up to feel that he belongs to the cultural group which rears him.

The teacher is also responsible for helping the child to become a member of society through learning what it means to become a social being, and a unique opportunity is offered by the school, which can create a social group to which the child can belong. Education is a group process, for children learn from other people and amongst other people, and we do not cultivate the individual to a point of separating him from his colleagues. The individual knows his unique qualities only in relation to others in the group, and it would be a pity if education led to isolation by concentrating exclusively on the development of the individual. Man is a social being, and the health of society depends on the mutuality of its members. Child-centred education does not mean education which is dominated by the separateness of the individual, but education which relates the individual to his fellows.

This aspect of the teacher's work is further complicated by the pluralistic nature of our present-day society. In many schools immigrant children introduce a great variety of cultural traditions, religious customs, dietary habits, and patterns of family life. Unless the teacher knows something of these differing backgrounds she is not able to understand the behaviour and ideas of these children. Language is a serious problem, but a teacher does not solve the immigrant problem by teaching the children to speak English. As immigrants become integrated into the community, they change it. British as well as immigrant children therefore need a multicultural education.

A teacher cannot assume that her own cultural background necessarily makes sense to the children she teaches. Young teachers are frequently deeply shaken when they come up against values and beliefs which run contrary to their own. For example, we cannot expect the child who has been brought up in a home where the satisfaction of the moment is of first importance to welcome the middle-class belief in relinquishing immediate gain for the sake of a future goal; the child who has never known possessions which are exclusively his own has little respect for the sanctity of private property, and the child who has learned to avoid physical pain by distorting the truth understands little of the value of honesty.

In a situation of this kind the teacher can do one of two things: she can pretend that the situation doesn't exist and try to train the child to conform to an unfamiliar social pattern; or she can make herself thoroughly conversant with the child's background and with the habits of thought prevalent amongst the adults who rear him, and can then help him to understand that there are other ways of living by introducing him to values which may bring him more permanent satisfaction.

A school functions as a small community set in a particular neighbourhood, which itself is part of a total and very complex society. Outside his immediate home circle, the teacher is the child's first link with the 'great society'. It is only by helping him to understand his own background and to adjust to the miniature society of the school that the teacher can eventually show the child what society is all about.

In one class none of the children would play with Gail. She was sullen and spiteful, snatched what she wanted and was always ready to tell tales. At home Gail was the only girl in a family of five. Her mother doted on her sons and Gail was a drudge to the other children.

Gail's teacher knew the family and understood the child's unhappy situation. She tried to help her to feel needed and important by giving her small responsibilities such as feeding the hamster or checking the milk bottles. She tried to show her that helping other people was rewarding and that doing things for the rest of the class could be a pleasure and need not be drudgery. As Gail became more acceptable to the other children, their growing friendliness opened up for her a new way of relating herself to others in the group. She was slowly learning how to live with other people as friends, and this was an experience which she had never been offered at home.

The teacher of the future will possibly become a social worker rather than someone whose main interest is in the intellectual development of the child, and the present-day emphasis on parent-teacher communication supports this view of her. If this is so, then the teacher will need to become a socially educated person and at least two radical changes in the habits of teachers will follow.

Colleges of Education tend to work in isolation and concentrate on educating for a single profession. In the words of the Plowden Report: 'A choice of career is forced on students at 18 or earlier, before some of them know their own minds, and future teachers are segregated from those preparing for other types of work' (para. 958). 'We hope there may be some situations in which social service students and students preparing for teaching can share much of their first year work, especially as this should encourage closer collaboration in the field. . . . We also welcome experiments now about to be put into effect for training teachers in selected technical colleges, especially because they will increase the opportunities of prospective teachers to train side by side with students in other disciplines who are preparing for other professions' (para. 960). The social isolation of the teacher in training is contrary to the concept of the teacher as a social worker, and we await with interest the results of experiments already launched in this field. At present the whole question of teacher training is under review, and many interesting ideas may emerge from this controversy.

There is also a tendency amongst teachers to make friends mainly with teachers or others in their own profession, and this can lead to a narrowing view of society. The teacher of the future will need to become a member of society in the fullest possible sense of the word, if she is to fulfil her responsibility to children. It will become increasingly important for her to relinquish the traditional authoritarian concept of her role in order to become a person who can listen to the problems of others and can help them to talk out their worries in much the same way as the social worker treats people in distress.

11

The partnership between parents and teachers

Perhaps the most persistent and important principle which emerges from a study of child development is the wholeness of the individual and the continuity of the way in which he learns. We can no longer consider the work we do with the child in school as separate from what happens to him outside it: the two aspects of the child's world must work together in harmony if he is to develop as he should.

The significance of the continuous interaction between home and school is given priorty in the Plowden Report. Research emphasises the influence of parental attitudes upon educational performance, and 'one of the essentials for educational advance is closer partnership between the two parties to every child's education' (para. 102).

In recent years parents have taken a growing interest in what happens to their children in school. Parents are now held responsible by law for the adequate education of their children, and they have never been so well informed about the aims and procedures of the schools which their children attend. They know that money for education comes out of their own pockets and they grow increasingly confident in their ability to get value for their money. A number of associations, e.g. the Confederation of Associations for the Advancement of State Education (C.A.S.E.), have been established to support and further the views of parents.

In some cases, however, increasing but still limited knowledge of children and their educational needs has made parents feel uncertain about their responsibilities. There are many parents today who are almost afraid to bring their children up because of what they might do to them; parental instincts are suspect and treatment of offspring must follow the rules of 'child psychology'. This conflict in attitude between a growing sense of interest and responsibility and a growing sense of uncertainty and lack of confidence has a profound effect on the relationship between home and school, and teachers must understand the diffidence of parents in order to help them to overcome it.

Research projects and government reports have proved the value to the child of a middle-class background. J. W. B. Douglas based the observations he makes in *The Home and the School* (MacGibbon and Kee, 1964) on a study of 5,000 children born in 1946. He points out that children of middle-class parents get the same proportion of Grammar School places one would expect from their ability, while only 52 per cent of the places expected from their ability are gained by children of lower manual workers. The conclusion he draws is that parental attitudes matter more to the child than any other single factor. It isn't so much that working-class parents don't care about their children, but that their apathetic attitude signifies their inability to overcome the odds against them and they readily become resigned to what they consider to be their lot.

Elsie was the eldest in a family of five. Their home consisted of 'an up and a down' in a terrace of back-to-back houses. They shared a strip of yard and a midden with a neighbour. Elsie gained a Grammar School place, and on the morning she received the news she went to the headmaster and told him that she didn't want to take the place.

'That's a pity,' the headmaster replied: 'You're a clever girl and you'd enjoy the new things you'd learn in the Grammar School. Why don't you want to go, Elsie?'

Elsie answered simply: 'Well, sir. I'd make new friends and I couldn't bring them home, could I? Besides, I'd have nowhere to do my homework.'

When one parent learned that her child had taken the 11 + tests, she wrote to the headmaster. 'Please don't put our

77

Joanna's name down for the Grammar School, I don't want her to have ideas above her station.'

These unfortunate attitudes persist as much through lack of communication as through difficult circumstances, for parents fear what they don't understand. Their ideas about education are rooted in the experiences of early childhood, and there is a great deal which teachers can do to revise these ideas and to help parents to develop more favourable impressions of school and of what education can do for their children. Antagonistic parents need help, not abuse or criticism, but even when a parent enters a friendly school he may still respond to the situation with the emotional habits he learned as a child, and may need a lot of encouragement before he can develop new emotional habits. Communication with him must be at a personal level, and a talk given by the head to a crowd of parents may not reach him at all.

Good work has been done by such associations as C.A.S.E. and Parent-Teacher Associations, but these in themselves are not necessarily solutions to the problem. Many teachers have found that communication at a personal level between individual parents and teachers is the only really effective means of helping parents to adjust their attitudes and to develop true and active co-operation.

This doesn't mean, however, that the teacher must always fall over backwards in order to win support from a parent: sometimes it means taking a firm line.

Terry's teacher suspected that Terry was slightly spastic. He was clumsy; his movements were unco-ordinated, and he found written work a problem. At the age of eight he was losing confidence, and because he was intelligent, he was fully conscious of the gap between his attainments and those of his friends. His mother was a timid woman and very evasive. 'You'd better speak to his father about it,' she said, when gently questioned: 'My husband's in business and he wants Terry to take over when he grows up. He has ideas about Terry's education and I don't have much say in the matter.'

As Terry's father was never free during the day, the headmistress arranged to see him one evening. 'There's nothing wrong with Terry,' the father persisted: 'He was brought up in a flat and we had to keep him quiet. He didn't get much chance to run about and play before he came into school and it's made him a bit clumsy in his movements. He'll grow out of it.'

The father was obviously ambitious for his son. As an intelligent and well-built man himself, he was not prepared to face the fact that there could be something wrong with Terry. Terry admired his father, and this increased his feeling of inadequacy. His growing conflict was an additional handicap, and tension reduced his powers of co-ordination.

Eventually the headmistress took matters into her own hands and wrote to the father. 'I am convinced,' she explained, 'that Terry needs medical attention. I have recommended him for special examination when the School Medical Officer visits at the end of the term, and I hope you will feel able to attend.'

She received no reply to the letter, but Terry's father turned up on the appointed day—her forthright action had shaken him. This was the first step towards a more realistic attitude on his part, and Terry was allowed to receive the medical attention he needed. When Terry left the school, his father came to see the headmistress. 'I'm sorry he's moving up,' he said: 'He's come on a lot in this school. Thank you for all you've done for him.' He was acknowledging his recognition of her genuine concern for his son's welfare and the fact that she had made him examine his own attitude towards him.

Dr Kellmer Pringle, in the report *11,000 Seven-year-olds* (Longmans, 1966) points out an interesting relationship between the lead taken by parents in initiating discussion with teachers about their children, and the occupations of those parents. Generally speaking, parents in the lower sociometric groups rarely approach the school to discuss the educational progress of their children. Many teachers would confirm this fact and would add some comment to the effect that these same parents are difficult to entice into school at all.

job.' The reply to this was: 'She's the eldest of seven, and she's had to share from the start. She's a bit slow and a proper butterfingers, and Dad shouts his head off if she breaks anything.'

In one school the headmistress has organised a Mothers' Club, which meets once a fortnight to discuss with her, or a member of staff, and sometimes a visiting speaker, some aspect of child development or of the way in which children learn in the school and home. Mothers who are members of this club offer their services to the school when a suitable occasion arises. Once a year they spend a day out with the teachers, leaving the children in the care of their fathers. For a few of the mothers this may be the only day in the year when they leave their domestic responsibilities behind. It is a day which all concerned enjoy very much.

Some teachers make a routine visit to the homes of the children at least once during the year, but the majority of teachers feel that the home visit is more welcomed when a specific occasion arises, e.g. when a child is taken ill in school and the teacher either accompanies him home or calls later to enquire about his welfare.

This kind of work involves teachers in the expenditure of personal time, and yet most of them feel that it is time well spent. Attitudes can be changed, and teachers can change them.

12

The teacher and the student

How does the teacher view the student? Is she an additional burden, a second pair of hands or an investment in the future? Could students be trained without teaching practice? Could we leave all training to the schools? Are colleges and schools on opposite sides of the fence, or are they 'yolked together'? (Plowden Report, para. 984.) Is it possible to cultivate a more fruitful partnership between schools and colleges? What part does the class teacher play in providing the teachers of the future?

Many practising teachers can remember the time when the allocation of a student was considered to be an honour. Colleges had few students to place. Local Authorities recommended those schools which they considered eligible to participate in the training of teachers, and it was to the more experienced and able teachers that a student was allocated.

The rapid expansion of colleges has intensified the use of schools for practice and observation. Schools are asked to receive students more frequently and for longer periods, and what was once considered an honour is now sometimes seen as a nuisance. A few schools have even tried to close their doors to students altogether. It is the class teachers themselves who can resolve the situation, for, in placing students, head teachers are dependent on the goodwill of teachers and tend to take their lead from them.

The teacher of young children has an advantage, when dealing with students, over her colleagues in the Secondary School. As a general practitioner she remains with the same group of children for most of the day, and she therefore sees a student handling an unchanging group of children and is able to observe her performance in every type of situation. She is in a much better position to help the student than the Secondary teacher, who may see the student for perhaps two to eight periods per week, during which time she is meeting anything up to two hundred children.

But the Primary situation also produces the teacher's most difficult problem: she is expected to relinquish her class to a stranger who may differ very much from herself in temperament and whose ways of doing things may seem to be at cross-purposes with her own. The student's need to take over the class varies, of course, according to her skill and experience. Some students show an aptitude for meeting the needs of children right from the start. Others, unfortunately, are slower learners, and a student may be into her third period of practice before she is confident enough to take complete charge of a class for any length of time. Sometimes the teacher is faced with a student who seems to have no aptitude at all for the job, or one whose lack of personal confidence is so acute that she finds great difficulty in fulfilling her own potential while handling someone else's class.

There are a number of ways in which school-based experience for students is organised, but teaching practice is the most familiar and widely operated. We will examine the teaching practice to begin with, and then consider other ways in which teachers and students can co-operate for the benefit of children as well as of the student.

It may be as well to start by recognising the artificial nature of the teaching practice situation. The student is expected to adjust to a situation organised and run by another person. At the same time she is assessed largely on her contribution, and her major problem is how to exercise her own skill without conflicting with a way of working which has already been established between a group of children and this other highly influential person in charge of them. The class can never be hers, however generous the teacher may be, and she has little actual responsibility for it. The student is not employed by the Local

Authority and is therefore not insured, so that it is impossible, however willing the class teacher may be, to hand over ultimate responsibility to her. For instance, if the student wishes to take a group of children to visit the local bakery, the class teacher, or some other insured person, must accompany her. Any planning the student does is within the framework of another person's responsibility, and she can never feel fully in charge of her own affairs.

Many teachers realise this, and sometimes try to remedy the situation by removing themselves and their influence as drastically as possible from the classroom. 'I've stripped the walls,' they explain to the student: 'You can create your own environment and I want you to try out all the ideas they've suggested at college.'

This is a very generous gesture, and the teacher may be objective enough about her job to feel that, as she has encouraged her children to learn from every situation, they will at least learn something from what the student prepares, and may learn something which she herself had never thought of offering.

Unfortunately this rarely works. Children find it difficult to adjust quickly to a completely fresh environment as well as to a fresh teacher-figure. Also, many of the activities which they have shared with their teacher are suddenly terminated, and the continuity of the learning process is further disrupted when the student leaves and takes her environment with her.

The most helpful gesture a teacher can make is to allow the student to work alongside her, making two sets of ears, two pairs of hands and two minds available to the children. If she can provide one clear display corner in which the student can introduce some of her own material, this gives her a good start.

The student can increase her responsibility in several ways: she can supervise certain activities and gradually add to these; she can take full charge for a period of time each day and gradually increase its length; she can be given a group of children with whom to work more intimately and, as she develops, she can increase the size of the group or the number of small groups. In this way continuity is ensured for the children, and the student's responsibility can be adjusted to correspond to her aptitude.

Easing the student into the situation should begin before the actual practice, and many teachers can make use of an able person, often young and full of life, on several occasions in advance of the practice proper. Visits, open days and school functions are all times when an extra person is useful, and if the student can be made to feel of use to the community well in advance of the practice, this adds to her establishment as part of the school and is more helpful than mere 'observation'.

During the practice the teacher should feel free to discuss the student's work with her, to offer advice and criticism, to make positive suggestions and to take a recognised share in the supervision and assessment of the student's work. The student's file should be included in the supervisory duties of the teacher. It is not a secret document which only the college tutor should read.

In some colleges final assessment of the student includes conferences between tutor, class teacher and head teacher, with opportunity for the student to discuss her own performance. The class teacher should always feel that she is the king-pin in the operation: indeed, students cannot be told by their tutors how to teach, they can only learn this from experience with children and their teachers in the classroom. The responsibility of the college is to prepare the student, both by study of children and by specific preparation for the practice, to make the best possible use of the learning opportunity that teaching practice affords.

Two major worries of the teacher—whether the inexperienced person will be able to handle the children and a fear of the class 'going to pieces'—account for the resistance of some teachers to student practice. Part of the problem lies in the fact that a student cannot learn about the control of children until she is left in control. She may learn much by observing the way in which the expert encourages the development of personal discipline in young children, but she cannot discover by mere observation how she will do what seems so easily achieved by the experienced person.

It takes a great deal of courage on the part of the teacher to watch another person learn from the mistakes she makes when handling a class which the teacher regards as her own creation. One teacher dealt with the situation in the following way.

On her second practice Sarah was allocated to a class of six- to seven-year-old children. Their teacher, Miss Raymond, gave Sarah her record book. 'You can spend these first two days,' she said, 'talking to individual children and getting to know their names. My notes may help you to discover something about them. On Wednesday you can take over for the last hour in the morning. Let the children tell you about the things they are doing. Find time to show them one or two of those interesting working toys you're going to explore with them later on in the week. I'll come in and check the dinner tickets, but you can get the children ready to go home. The helper will fetch the dinner children at five to twelve.' In this way she eased Sarah into the situation and showed her the importance of knowing children as individuals before expecting to handle them as a group.

School-based experience for students is largely initiated by the colleges. Observation, the exploration of ideas in subjects such as mathematics and science by working with groups of children, the use of clinical tests, team-teaching involving tutors and students and, occasionally, associating individual students with individual children, are some of the more popular ways of helping students to relate theoretical aspects of their course to the child situation.

Sometimes a dual appointment opens up the possibilities. In one college a tutor works there for half the week and in a Primary School for the other half. His school responsibility, as a part-time teacher, is to provide extended experience for slower learning children of eight or nine, and he enlists the assistance of students, finding them of particular use in helping children to develop linguistic skill. Individual students are attached to individual children; they encourage the children to talk freely, help them with their reading and writing problems, and generally attempt to build up their linguistic confidence.

In another college, a tutor responsible for an education group and a teacher from a neighbouring school work together. Each student in the tutor's group is attached to a child in the teacher's class. The student visits the child in school about twice each term and keeps a record of many aspects of the child's development. In between these visits the student arranges contact with the child in a number of ways. Some take a group of children to the local zoo; others offer their services as child-sitters in the child's own home. Sometimes the teacher brings the class to the college, where the students organise activities for them, e.g. movement, exploration of new equipment, scientific investigation, and so on.

Only occasionally is an activity of this kind initiated by a teacher, but if, in fact, teachers are to take joint responsibility with tutors in colleges for the training of future teachers, then initiative should come as much from the teacher as from the college tutor.

The following examples may suggest possible lines of development in building up a fully adequate relationship between schools and colleges.

Teachers from one school asked to visit the college. A tutor met them, entertained them for tea and conducted them round the college, discussing with them some of the amenities. As a result of this visit the teachers were invited to use the college library whenever they wished. On another occasion the head-mistress of the same school arranged for members of the school's Mothers' Club to visit the college. Students showed them round, and over a cup of tea talked to them about their college course. The teachers in the school later discussed with the mothers their impressions of student training.

There are, of course, a number of links forged between

teachers and colleges through the work of local organisers and through arrangements made by colleges to involve teachers in teaching practice exercises and in taking an active part in the students' courses by giving talks, lending the work of children, and so on.

Again it is refreshing to explore ideas promoted by the teachers themselves. One teacher offered to lend examples of the work of her children at different times in the year for display in the college workshop. Her display included a cleverly designed frieze which described, with appropriate examples, the way in which she encouraged creative writing, from the children's first attempts at scribbling to the achievement of a story.

Liaison between practising teachers and teachers in training is improving. Yet much remains to be done, and the individual teacher can offer valuable service in this field.

13

The teacher as a leader

Modern conceptions of the educational development of young children have transformed the relationship between teacher and child. The teacher has always been a leader of the young, and authority is an essential factor in the educational process, but the teacher who instructs and directs has given way to the teacher who advises and inspires.

Rousseau believed that teaching 'is a question of guidance rather than instruction'. We no longer see the teacher as an instructor in combat with unwilling minds, but as a leader who enables the child to learn from what he does rather than from what is done to him. Authoritarian forms of leadership, in which the teacher dominates have been replaced by leadership through suggestion, stimulation and example, but the new form of leadership is more difficult to maintain, depending on personal qualities rather than on personal power.

A teacher cannot avoid leadership. As a more experienced and mature person she has taken, along with the job, the duty of leading her pupils towards intellectual and moral responsibility, and she 'teaches' as much by attitude as by anything else. Her duties of leadership in the school community involve her in working with caretakers and maintenance staff, auxiliary staff and teachers' aides, and students and parents, as part of her immediate circle, while other members of society within which the school operates may turn to her for leadership too. During the Middle and Secondary years of schooling, the teacher may be required to participate in team-teaching projects, taking the lead according to her particular strength. In every type of school the teacher works as part of a staff team, and an effective team involves each of its members in leadership. As a leader in the staff team, the teacher must be capable of initiating and planning for the group, of involving the less-experienced members of staff in a worthwhile capacity, and of offering her own experience in the service of the whole community.

Leadership, then, functions in a number of ways, and we shall now examine two aspects of leadership which more directly concern the teacher of young children. We will look first at the way in which the class teacher leads the children for whom she is directly responsible, and then we will consider the way in which leadership operates in team-teaching with children from both the First and Middle School range.

The teacher's capacity to inspire children is her most influential and benevolent form of leading them. The teacher who possesses a scintillating personality would seem to have an advantage, and her quieter colleague might envy her. Observation of teachers, however, leads one to believe that the teacher who works hard to provide inspiration often succeeds more consistently than the scintillating person whose gift may tend to fluctuate. Inspiration depends more on personal enthusiasm than it does on ecstatic moods. It is not metaphysical and no teacher need lack it. Inspiration can be cultivated, and most teachers can be inspirational to children.

A starting-point is personal interest, and we have already discussed ways in which a teacher can use her own enthusiasms to stimulate interest in children. Personal interest leads to involvement, and allowing oneself to become involved is a personal habit which can be cultivated. The teacher who readily becomes involved in what catches a child's interest can share the burning enthusiasm of the child when he is absorbed. She and the child are caught up in a common pursuit, and in this state of heightened sensitivity mind stimulates mind, each individual involved discovering the full extent of his personal capacity.

Interest itself is not a fickle quality. It comes as a result of effort, and the dullest child can reveal unexpected depths when a teacher makes the effort to be interested in him and in what is going on in his mind.

These attitudes, coupled with willingness on the part of the teacher to ensure that materials are in good supply, in good condition and exciting in their variety, will produce conditions which inspire, because the activation of the child to communicate is associated with adequate means of expression. These principles were behind the work of one teacher.

Miss Cooper was a sensitive person who appreciated the creative work of others. She was not particularly creative with materials herself, and recognised the aridity of her own childhood education in limiting her opportunity to explore the creative use of paint, clay and fabrics. The children in her class came from homes where parents had neither the aptitude nor the energy to do more than keep the family going, and music, art and poetry were considered to be the extravagance of the idle rich.

Miss Cooper provided many materials and was most disappointed with the unimaginative efforts of the children. She then realised that she was expecting them to express feelings and experiences which they had never had; 'how can these children make exciting pictures,' she thought, 'when life has only introduced them to dull experiences in shabby homes?' She realised that their lack of imagination hampered them in every aspect of learning, and she concentrated on providing them with mental images which would form the raw material of imagination. She read them the poems she loved herself. She collected unusual and exotic fabrics. She took some of them to a local art gallery and two of them to see a ballet. She brought her own precious records to school. She took them round a stately home and to a local museum, and invited members of the local actors' workshop to visit the children in school. She took some of them home and served them with tea from her best tea-service. She also made sure that there was fresh, clear paint in the painting corner and that the clay was pleasant to handle. She provided all she could to encourage creative work, but she didn't demand it of them.

Six months of the year passed and there was little to show. She had apparently neglected academic work in order to enrich the lives of these children and she began to wonder whether her efforts had been wasted. The Easter holiday came and she spent an uneasy time wondering how she was going to catch up with the reading and mathematics.

On their return to school the children showed an unexpected interest in their materials. Their first tentative efforts took on a sudden vigour, and an upsurge of creative work spread through the group. It was as though they were sparked into life, and the spark spread to academic aspects of their work. Each child was working at full stretch.

Sometimes teachers feel that the children have settled into a rut, or they take over a new class and wish to make a change towards a more liberal way of working. A teacher in such a situation feels the need to 'take the lead'. She is experienced enough to know that drastic measures lead to disaster, and wishes the change-over to be as smooth and profitable as possible, so she starts in quite a small way.

A difficult situation may arise when a headmistress, who is anxious to develop her school along more flexible lines but unwilling to disturb the main body of her staff, says to the more adventurous members or to the young idealist fresh from college, 'You can have a free hand. Plan your class in any way you wish. I am most interested in seeing these new ideas in action.' She may add, 'And I'll back you up', but this does not remove the great problem of trying to work out of step with the rest of the school.

The victim of such a decision would be well advised to proceed with caution. Children and adults need ample time to adjust and can only accommodate themselves to small doses of the unfamiliar, particularly during the early stages.

A gradual change towards a more liberal way of working

can be effected in several ways. One teacher established an investigation corner, where a group of more able children could work for a whole morning while she carried on with the rest of the class. As this group became independent, she introduced a second group to mathematical activities. Gradually she established a number of small groups, each working with material they were capable of handling. Later the groups began to merge and the work became more integrated.

Another teacher introduced a number of activities in bays round the room. As the children completed the work she wanted them to do, they were free to choose from the interests available. Many of these self-chosen jobs provided mathematical and linguistic problems, and as the teacher became more confident that 3R work was adequately catered for in a free approach, she reduced the amount of time spent on class teaching.

The function of a leader in a team project varies according to the age-group of the children, but the general principles apply in any situation. Leadership depends on the particular aptitude which qualifies a teacher to lead, and this usually means that she is required to offer her services as a specialist to the whole of the team. Where young children are concerned, this may simply mean that they associate certain types of activity with individual teachers. Mrs West is fond of cooking and this seems to take place every day in her classroom. Miss Gordon is artistic and provides very exciting materials; painting in her room is a constant adventure. Mrs Pickering loves poetry and has, in her special book, a wonderful collection of poems to which children love to listen. Where children are free to move from room to room, the specialist interests of teachers are available to any child in the school.

Members of a staff team may prepare to develop fresh interests in a school by discussion and by studying together. One teacher took a science degree before she trained for Primary School teaching; she led staff discussion on ways of initiating scientific exploration, and collected suitable reference books for the classroom libraries. Another teacher with a flair for musical composition introduced members of staff to simple ways in which children could be helped to record their own musical composition, and she sent away for catalogues and prepared an order for the headmistress. The lovely wooden musical instruments she introduced into the school were a source of great joy and inspiration to both the children and their teachers.

In the Middle School age ranges a member of staff may introduce a topic to a large group of children and their teachers. Her preparation and presentation need to be very good indeed, because they provide the framework of the course of study which several class groups will follow. Children and teachers then break up into smaller groups for discussion. Individual children, or small groups of children, will take up associated lines of study, and some children may need individual tutorials from their teachers.

This procedure makes heavy demands on the specialist. In Middle and Upper Schools the teacher's specialist qualification establishes his or her standing on the staff. He has been appointed because of it, and it takes a great deal of courage to renounce one's standing and view specialist work as part of a larger pattern. Unless all members of staff are equally generous, team-teaching cannot work.

It is equally difficult for the specialist to reconcile himself to the idea that he no longer teaches a subject but guides children in self-chosen pursuits which may stem from a subject interest but may then branch out in many directions. Team-teaching of an integrated or combined course for a group of children requires complete reorientation of the way in which a teacher views his job. The Primary and the Secondary teacher can learn much from one another, and it is in a synthesis of their aims and ideals that the future success of Middle School teaching lies.

Under any circumstances, team-work depends on the enthusiasm of its members. Where new ideas are promoted, it is usually through a group of enthusiasts who pool their resources, and the success of these ideas depends on the sustained interest of the group. An interesting feature of group projects is the way in which the work changes as a result of a change in the team. Leadership does not necessarily mean that one leads and the others follow, for the most effective team-work develops when a group of people can share the lead, each initiating or following as the situation demands. The motivation of the group lies in a project which is more important than the interests of any single member, and leadership functions in the service of all to the group project.

14

The teacher as a learner

The initial training of a teacher is only an introduction. Learning about the job and about children will continue until the day the teacher retires. Some teachers carry on learning about the job even after retirement.

One quality of education is that it changes. The child's main role in life is to acquaint himself with his environment and to make his contribution to it, and each individual is partly responsible for the changes which take place in any environment. There are always fresh avenues to explore and fresh ways of exploring them: the child of today would feel ill equipped to understand the beautiful sapphire image of earth as seen from a spacecraft if his educational diet were restricted to what his parents had learned at his age.

Teachers are educating children for the world of tomorrow. Information which reaches the schools is always a few stages behind current events and developments, and teachers have discovered the value of cultivating the spirit of enquiry in children, rather than persisting in clogging their minds with facts, many of which become obsolete as soon as they are learned.

Vigorous research is extending Man's understanding of the functions of his own body, and yet comparatively little is known about the human brain and about the learning process. This means that constant revision of procedures is imperative. The fact that a method 'works' is no proof that a more effective procedure could not be found to take its place. Primary education has made rapid strides in this country, but little of it is based on clinically devised educational theory. The teacher of young children tends to work intuitively, for she is very close to her children and sensitive to their needs. She does what she does because *she* senses it is right, rather than because the psychologist has told her it is. She finds support in the findings of research workers, but she doesn't wait for them to suggest what she should do.

An inspired observation recorded in the Plowden Report crystallises this situation: 'What is immediately needed is that teachers should bring to bear in their day-to-day problems astringent intellectual scrutiny' (para. 550). The teacher is always seeking ways of improving her skill, and the more involved she becomes in helping children to learn, the more involved she becomes in being a learner herself.

There are many teachers in Primary Schools who are learning other roles in addition to that of being a teacher. A large proportion of teachers in Infant Schools are married women; many of them have children of their own and are learning how to be teachers, housewives, mothers and, even, grandparents. Each of these separate roles contributes to their learning. Motherhood has added a fresh dimension to the work of many teachers. As one married teacher returner said, 'Before, I did the job and enjoyed the children, but since I've had children of my own, I feel I know so much more about them, and now I'm far more interested in the children than in doing the job.'

What opportunities are there for the teacher as a learner? The Plowden Report offers a clear and concise account of in-service training facilities in paragraphs 1013-1027, and many LEAs try to ensure that teachers attend some form of in-service training at regular intervals. What teachers gain from these courses varies enormously, and it is certainly true to say that compulsory attendance creates a far less helpful situation than one finds on a course for which teachers have voluntarily applied.

Perhaps the most successful courses are those which are organised by teachers for teachers. One teachers' society insists on paying for its own courses, thus retaining the power to determine their direction. Local Authority personnel are members of the society but have no more power than any other teacher to determine a course; they work alongside the teachers in organising courses, but they are not in a position to use the society merely to forward their own ideas. The balance between the practising teacher and the promotion of educational practice is very profitably maintained in a society of this kind.

Many LEAs have helped teachers to organise their own centres where lectures and discussion groups, together with good library facilities, keep teachers abreast of developments. Some centres have established a teachers' workshop. Here teachers are provided with wood and other materials, and a skilled instructor. They attend the workshop each week and make equipment such as bookshelves, dividers, record cabinets and tables for use in their own classrooms. In a situation such as this, teachers are not only making useful equipment to help them in their job, but they are also learning how to handle fresh materials and to become more aware of the problems which face children when they first work with unfamiliar materials.

In other workshops teachers have the opportunity to explore a large range of teaching aids. A course of instruction in the use of projectors, tape-recorders, cameras, and the possibilities of C.C.T.V., radio and videotape, enable many who are not technically minded to overcome their fears of such equipment and to see its possible uses for extending communication in the classroom.

Libraries are, of course, a very helpful source of information, and a good librarian will guide teachers in their study of recent research. But the teacher is fundamentally a person who owns books rather than borrows them, and a well-stocked personal library is the stock-in-trade of the teacher who treats her job as an art as well as a skill. In one school the members of staff each contributed 5s and a small library of recent paperbacks was purchased. These were circulated for reading and were then kept in a bookcase in the staff room for reference. In another school, educational periodicals are made available to all members of staff in a similar way at a low cost to each.

There are, of course, a few treasured books that each teacher accumulates during the course of experience. Many educational truths hold good from generation to generation, and well-written books which embody these truths form a teacher's bible and offer refreshment and inspiration through many years of teaching. Such a library depends very much on personal choice. A writer who can articulate the truths which lie 'half asleep in the dawning of your own knowledge' becomes a friend and a guide, and his wisdom 'leads you to the threshold of your own mind'. (From *The Prophet* by Kahlil Gibran. Heinemann, 1926.) A short list of books which many teachers have found useful can be found at the end of this book.

The most important source of learning for the teacher is, of course, the child. Revised educational practice emphasises the importance of the relationship between teacher and child. The learning situation becomes an extremely intimate one in which teacher and child communicate at a very deep personal level, and their sensitivity to one another enriches the lives of both. The teacher senses the needs and reactions of children as individuals, while the child senses and reacts to the sympathy and understanding of the teacher who accepts him. He is extremely perceptive at an emotional level and readily senses the genuine or the sham; he knows his teacher's moods and temperament; he uncovers her strengths and her weaknesses, and he reaches her innermost spirit and calls upon it to strengthen his own.

In such a close relationship the teacher learns at first hand the implications of individual differences. She discovers the problems which face children in their attempts to learn. She learns that children can reason, although the way in which they do so is their own and not like that of an adult. They are her education and it is they who teach her how to teach.

The teacher learns *from* her children, and she also learns *with* them. A teacher no longer feels the need to be a paragon of knowledge; she doesn't mind admitting that she doesn't know something and that she can make mistakes. She is willing to share the adventure of learning with the child, and teacher and children often go hand-in-hand exploring undiscovered territories together. The teacher also encourages the child to formulate a point of view and to hold an opinion, and when she has helped him to express his opinion, she respects it.

It is in her capacity as a learner that the teacher enters into the closest communion with the child. She and the child are one, and the feeling of unity they both experience is in complete antithesis to the concept of compulsion in education which typified education in the traditional school. Co-operation and union take the place of rebelliousness and subordination, and the present-day freedom in communication generates a glorious freedom of spirit.

Teacher and child face one another as individuals who are eager to participate in the discovery of one another and in the discovery of life around them, and they stimulate one another to learn. The purpose of life in school for the teacher is the child, and the pivot of life in school for the child is the teacher.

'Thus he (the teacher) learns his responsibility for the particle of life entrusted to his care, and as he learns he educates himself. . . . The education of the pupil is thus always the self-education of the teacher.' (From *Education Through Art* by Herbert Read. Faber, 1958.)

15

The head teacher

So far in this book, the head teacher has been referred to only as a member of the staff team, and the question arises, has the head teacher a unique role to play in the education of young children?

At the moment, our system offers little in the way of specific training for headship and it is generally assumed that if the 'right' person is appointed to the job, the interpretation of her function can be left to her. Observation leads one to suppose that the interpretation of the role is very varied indeed and the ideas put forward in this chapter represent a very personal point of view. Nevertheless there is a certain consensus of agreement as to her function and while the role of the head teacher is even less clearly defined than that of the class teacher, some positive statements can be made.

In this country the role of head teacher carries a higher degree of authority than a comparable role in almost any other society. At the same time her authority depends on her willingness to accept many responsibilities. Once appointed, she is held responsible for virtually all that goes on in the school, yet no one dictates to her concerning either the running of the school or the type of education provided in it. Although from time to time school managers, local officials, parents, or sometimes even inspectors from the Department of Education and Science may make strong recommendations, they are not empowered to interfere in the way in which she carries out her job unless it can be proved that the children in her care are severely deprived educationally.

It would be difficult to give any order of priority to her

various responsibilities, for they overlap and are interdependent. It is, generally true to say, however, that the head teacher sees her role as one of leadership rather than one of administration. While she must administer for the smooth running of the school before she can exercise her powers of leadership, she never sees administration as an end in itself. Indeed, her powers of administration would probably be the least important of her qualifications for the job.

An obvious responsibility is to ensure for the school adequate provision of suitable equipment and materials. What she feeds into the environment becomes the lifeblood of learning, and a head teacher must be ever alert to what is available. The effect of introducing fresh and challenging material can be quite remarkable. Teachers and children will use what is to hand, and trends in the school are established through the materials in circulation. All members of staff can assist the head teacher in her selection of materials and some heads encourage members of staff to keep notebooks in which to make recommendations for the purchase of books, apparatus, equipment and materials.

Less tangible, but even more important, is the establishment in the school of an atmosphere in which teachers and children are encouraged to work as individuals in harmony with one another. The feeling which pervades a school stems partly from the personality of the head teacher and from the way of life in which she believes. It also depends on her willingness to take action in several definable ways.

She must first and foremost offer support to her staff. They will only feel free to experiment if she is prepared to take the ultimate responsibility for what happens as a result of experimentation. She must remain, under all circumstances, totally loyal to staff and children. She sets an example by working hard as a member of the staff team and by taking her full share of blame when things go wrong. She may need to criticise, even admonish from time to time, but this should be done with sympathy and compassion, and with a constant desire to see things from the other's point of view.

An important quality looked for in a head teacher is stability, for on her depends the security of all who work in the school. Sometimes, when things go astray or when conflict arises, a head teacher in her isolation can feel very much disturbed, even afraid. At such times she may need to make a semblance of confidence and make definite decisions even though she feels uncertain. Less harm is done by making an occasional mistake than by dithering when people are seeking guidance. Human beings can forgive mistakes, but they cannot tolerate a state of perpetual insecurity.

Perhaps the most important of her functions is the development of an appropriate philosophy in the school. This is a process rather than a set of ideas. It is not something thought up by the head and imposed on teachers and children. It is a way of life which develops from the harmonious working of all involved. It starts when the head teacher makes a sincere attempt to know and understand not only the adults and children in the school community, but the circumstances in which the school operates. She encourages all concerned to involve themselves in this same study, and she remembers to include parents, caretakers and all ancillary workers.

What evolves is unique in each school situation and the head teacher who tries to borrow and use the philosophy of another school will miss what is best for her own. The head teacher who operates from her 'private' room will miss many opportunities which are offered to the one who remains 'on tap' to the whole school. It is unfortunate that in some smaller schools the head teacher is usually in charge of a class for part, or the whole of the day. Her availability to the rest of the school is severely curtailed and the possibility of enthusing and inspiring others is diminished.

One head teacher made a habit of discussing each aspect of the development of the school with her staff which met her for that purpose once a week. She made a point of living in the school, and administrative work was cleared from her desk before 9 o'clock each morning, so that she was free to circulate for much of the day. She discussed with children and adults, points which arose in the course of the work. At the end of each year she wrote up a summary of the aims of the school and made recommendations for the coming year. This review of events expanded and frequently changed direction. Action is rooted in thought and it is from the deep study of the job in hand that worthwhile procedure emerges.

Sometimes a head teacher may feel the need to effect changes in the school. Her ideas may run ahead of those of her colleagues. If she knows her staff and children well, much is communicated to them even though few words are spoken. What she believes in colours her attitude to what is happening, and it is often through her reaction to the behaviour of others that she makes powerful suggestions. It is rarely wise to tell other people what to do, although much good can result when a head teacher is prepared to discuss new ideas with her teachers.

Members of staff, anxious to co-operate, may ask, 'What do you want me to do about so and so?' The head teacher who can help the questioner to think out an answer to her own question encourages a sense of independence in her staff, and the teacher who is thrown back on her own resources almost invariably comes up with a better answer than another person could offer. Thus the head teacher may initiate and disseminate ideas, but the interpretation of those ideas must be left to the individual.

Change brought about in this way is very often a slow process, but the growth of educationally sound practice can never be hurried. However anxious a newly appointed head teacher may be to make her mark, however impressive a new idea may seem to be, nothing will be gained by directing people or rushing them into action.

The head teacher of today operates in an educational world where innovation seems to predominate. Research reports, new approaches, fresh techniques, books about every aspect of teaching and learning threaten to swamp teachers and schools. Selection becomes a problem and it is easy to retreat and work out the salvation of a school in isolation.

However inspired the ideas held by a head teacher may be, they are not self-sufficient. She needs to keep abreast of recent developments, to select at least some books or periodicals which help her to keep in touch with the ideas and findings of others. She needs, in other words, to reach out in thought and try to comprehend education as a universal concern. Her school is part of a national system and educational progress is of international significance. Each school can benefit from a critical consideration of new developments in education, and each school contributes to the total development of education in our times.

While the fostering of good relationships within the community is an obvious responsibility of the head teacher, it is not always so apparent that she is also responsible for forging links between the school and many other parts of society. Links between school and home have been paid much attention in recent years, but we must not forget that the school is also the child's first link with the wider world of many other groups and institutions. In some schools even the youngest children make regular visits to the local Old People's Home, neighbouring schools, factories, the theatre, museums and other cultural centres, and as they grow older, to other countries too. In nine cases out of ten it is the head teacher who initiates and organises these adventures into society, and by so doing helps children to become familiar with many forms of social activity.

While becoming thoroughly involved in the life of the school, the head teacher must remain to some extent detached from other members of the community. She is friendly with each member of staff and with parents, yet to form a close friendship with any one member of staff can put her in a difficult position, for she must remain objective in viewing the work of each member of her team. Nor can she allow herself to become too caught up in any particular aspect of the school enterprise. In order to maintain a balanced and harmonious community, the head teacher must remain in a position of critical observer and this often means that she is committed to a lonely but intensely interesting job.

Visitors to schools in this country are always struck by their great diversity, and perhaps nowhere is this more apparent than in the schools for younger children. Because early education depends very much on the personal relationships which exist within a school community, each individual affects the life of the school in a very positive way, and the head teacher at the core of the situation lends undeniable character to her school.

It seems amazing that so little is done about education for headship. In any other walk of life training for managerial posts is available, and many newly appointed head teachers feel the need for tuition at least in their capacity as administrators. To tell a head teacher how to develop her school could lead to uniformity which is foreign to our system, but to find head teachers expending precious energy learning how to budget requisition accounts, how to advise members of staff on their conditions of service, and how to complete complicated forms and make use of social services, surely indicates a gap in professional training.

In conclusion

If there is any general conclusion to be drawn from these reflections, it is that the teacher of young children today has a radically different role from that of her counterpart in the past. She is no longer seen merely as the preserver of knowledge, the transmitter of culture, the instructor in basic skills. She must be flexible in her thinking, able to accept and evaluate new ideas and to adjust her approach in the light of what she understands about the society in which she lives and works.

Nor can we define what her role shall be, for a fundamental of contemporary education is its personal nature; the individual shapes her role according to her unique personality. What she holds to be true about education is what will guide her in her work, and it is the first responsibility of any teacher to seek out her own philosophy. Personal conviction is her compass, and her own resources as a person determine the way in which children in her care can learn.

Child-centred education is not the antithesis of teacher-centred education, for while the child remains at the centre of the teacher's thoughts and aims in education, the teacher remains at the centre of the child's world in school.

Teacher's library

Castle, E. B. *The Teacher*. OUP, 1970.

Edmonds, E. L. *The First Headship*. Blackwell, 1968.

Gardner, D. E. M. *Experiment and Tradition in Primary Schools*. Methuen, 1966.

Gardner, D. E. M. and **Cass, J. E.** *The Role of the Teacher in the Infant and Nursery School*. Pergamon, 1965.

Gibran, Kahlil. *The Prophet*. Heinemann, 1926.

Hoyle, Eric. *The Role of the Teacher*. Routledge & Kegan Paul, 1969.

Marshall, Sybil. *An Experiment in Education*. OUP, 1963

Mellor, Edna. *Education through Experience in the Infant School Years*. Blackwell, 1950.

Read, Herbert. *Education Through Art*. Faber, 1958.

Reid, Louis Arnaud. *Philosophy and Education*. Heinemann, 1962.

Russell, Bertrand. *A History of Western Philosophy*. Allen & Unwin, 1954

Whitehead, A. N. *The Aims of Education*. Ernest Benn, 1962.

Also

The World of Children. Paul Hamlyn, 1966.

Children and their Primary Schools (The Plowden Report), Volume 1. HMSO, 1967.

11,000 Seven-year-olds. Longmans, 1966.

Research: some studies
of the role of the teacher

In addition to those books included in the *Teacher's Library*, the following works help to elucidate some aspects of the teacher's role. Not all of them make specific reference to the teacher in the Infant School, but the general principles considered are applicable in many situations. While the list is by no means complete, these works will provide readers with starting-points for a more detailed study of the many factors which affect the job of the teacher.

Adams, S. *Analysing the teacher's role*. In Educational Research, Vol. 12, No. 2, 1970, pp. 121-127.

Baird, C. L. *The role of the teacher of six and seven-year-old children*. M.Ed. thesis, University of Manchester, 1967. (Abstract in British Journal of Educational Psychology, Vol. 38, Pt. 3, 1968, pp. 323-324.)

Bradburn, E. *The teacher's role in the moral development of children in primary schools*. Ph.D. thesis, University of Liverpool, 1963-64.

Cohen, L. *An exploratory study of the teacher's role as perceived by head teachers, tutors and students in a training college*. M.Ed. dissertation, University of Liverpool, 1965.

Evans, R. *The 'image' of the teacher in the national press*. M.A. (Econ.) dissertation, University of Manchester, 1962-63.

Finlayson, D. S. and **Cohen, L.** *The teacher's role: a comparative study of the conceptions of college of education students and head teachers*. In British Journal of Educational Psychology, Vol. 37, Pt. 1, 1967, pp. 22-31.

Floud, J. *Teaching in the affluent society*. In British Journal of Sociology, Vol. 13, No. 4, 1962, pp. 299-308.

Gammage, P. G. *The perception of the social role of primary school teachers by parents, pupils and teachers*. M.Ed. thesis, Leicester University, 1966-67.

Kob, J. *Definition of the teacher's role*. In **Halsey, A. H.** and others. *Education, economy and society: a reader in the sociology of education*. Free Press, 1961, pp. 558-576.

Musgrove, F. and **Taylor, P. H.** *Teachers' and parents' conception of the teacher's role*. In British Journal of Educational Psychology, Vol. 35, Pt. 2, 1965, pp. 171-178.

Taylor, P. H. *Children's evaluations of the characteristics of the good teacher*. In British Journal of Educational Psychology, Vol. 32, Pt. 3, 1962, pp. 258-266.

Tropp, Asher. *The school teachers: the growth of the teaching profession in England and Wales from 1800 to the present day*. Heinemann, 1957.

Waller, Willard. *The sociology of teaching*. Wiley, 1932. (Refers to American schools.)

Westwood, L. J. *The role of the teacher—I*. In Educational Research, Vol. 9, No. 2, 1967, pp. 122-134.

Westwood, L. J. *The role of the teacher—II*, 1967, pp. 21-37.

Wison, Bryan R. *The teacher's role—a sociological analysis*. In British Journal of Sociology, Vol. 13, No. 1, 1962, pp. 15-32.

Index